CW01648016

Tales of an Anxiety Warrior

Overcoming lifelong anxiety without professional help

JEN GRIFFITHS

Tales of an Anxiety Warrior

Overcoming lifelong anxiety without professional help

First published in 2022

ISBN: 978-1-7396854-0-9

Independently published with the support of
TAUK Publishing

DEDICATION

I would like to dedicate this book to my husband. We've been together since I was twenty-one, and he has been there for me through all the ups and downs. My soulmate, our dream team. Three of us made it to that beautiful sunset, and it is indeed full of true love's bliss!

FOREWORD

I'm Jen, the Tropic Pianist Gamer. I'm a mum, a wife, and I run two businesses and two voluntary organisations. I was always known as the 'girl that got stuff done', but little did they know it was driven by anxiety. Professional help didn't get me anywhere, and I refused the pills, but when I found the resources I needed, I used that diligence and consistency to my advantage. I'm still known as the 'lady who gets stuff done', but I'm no longer fuelled by anxiety and perfectionism.

This isn't the first time I've told my story, but it is part of the process of overcoming my anxiety disorder. Initially, I was scared of everything and everyone. I put on a mask to get through things, but it was rare I could truly enjoy myself for fear of being judged.

My journey with storytelling started with a guest spot on a blog in August 2020, and after inspiring a few friends to talk about their mental health struggles, I set up my blog in May 2021 to tell my story. From that, I had the opportunity to join a collaboration for the best-selling book, *Seen.* I wrote the first chapter, which was significant to me as it was the first chapter to the rest of my story, and now is that time to tell the rest of the story.

Names have been changed to protect privacy.

RACISM IN RECEPTION

I remember being at primary school. I was subjected to racist bullying as young as reception year because I was mixed race, but back then, it was like water off a duck's back. My mum told me to ignore the bullies, which I did. If people mocked me for other things, I'd learn to mock them back. By year four, it was just banter then.

I was a happy kid; I was looked after. My dad had a decent job, and my mum stayed at home. I could get overconfident on occasion. I remember when a family friend brought me some flashy trainers for my birthday. I showed off at school, and I thought I was one of the big guys.

In years five and six, I just wanted to fit in, so I got in with a group of 'cool' girls. The kind of girls that thought it was acceptable to pick on kids that were different. We were only young then, but one kid used to sit with his hands down his pants, so we essentially ripped him to shreds (verbally). The irony was he used to be my best friend in year three; the friends I had in year five decided he was a weirdo and I just wanted to keep in with the group, so I didn't stick up for him either.

I would like to add that karma came back to bite me as we ended up at the same secondary school and the same friendship circle. One day he decided he'd had enough after I'd called him names, and he threw a drink over me as revenge, so that was the end of all the bullying!

I was good at quite a few things at primary school, though. I was on the football, rugby, and cricket teams. I'd done gymnastics for a short while, and I nearly did ballet. (An introductory session where I saw a girl crying when trying to do the splits put me off.) I was also on the chess team and was nearly the champion in year six, but I was so nervous I got beaten by fools' mate (the shortest checkmate in a chess game) in the final. I cried! I'm pretty sure my teacher or mum told me to get over it and stop being silly.

The other thing I was in was the recorder band. The recorder band was both a great opportunity and the bane of my life. I think it was year five, and the school production was *Hansel & Gretel*. I wanted to be the witch, so I auditioned. I thought my cackle was quite impressive, but it was given to the soppy kid with the arm sling as the headteacher told me I was better suited to the recorder band. Way to crush a child's dream! I never auditioned for anything acting-wise again after that.

All this sounds so negative, and although negativity ran rife through my childhood, I wouldn't say I had a bad childhood. My parents looked after me and my brother the best they could. They were anxious themselves. I can't judge them for that. However, I know this is where the very roots of my anxiety disorder started. They weren't just roots; they ran deep and had strong foundations. Anxiety was seen as 'normal' for a very long time, simply because I didn't know any different (and presumably neither did they.) There's still a stigma around mental health now, but it was unspoken, at least in my family. In the 80s/90s, I was just the shy kid with the puppy fat. I'd grow out of it. Except I didn't. It just got worse over time.

THE INVISIBLE TARGET

It was years eight to nine when things started to go wrong. I was getting bullied every single day. Was it karma? Well, maybe, and then some.

Fat, ugly, swot or geeky. I even got bullied in year nine because I had a boyfriend. I was bullied for shaving my legs when I hadn't even hit puberty. I then got bullied for having hairy legs. My mum never told me that girls didn't have hairy legs, as due to her side of the family not having that problem, the thought never occurred to her, so I didn't know I was supposed to remove the hair. I also had a dry type of follicular eczema since birth, which hampered my ability to remove hair properly. Over time I got the idea, but I had to put aside a whole afternoon just to sort my legs out. As a result, I just decided to wear tights as much as I could and hide away instead. Every little thing the bullies picked at, I tried to ignore, but it chipped away at me for several years.

Maybe I should have been grateful it never became physical. I heard that at the local comprehensive school it wasn't unusual to have your head shoved down the toilet. I was lucky that my parents sent me to a school out of the area as it was the nearest Church of England school, and I hoped that the kids would have more morals. Did they? At its worst, the bullying was led by a vicar's daughter. The irony!

But because I was older, I was the one who was accused of bullying because she looked so young and innocent. Her mother, the vicar, even went as far as to call me the devil incarnate! Yet it was her lovely daughter that used to taunt me on the school bus and throw chewing gum at my hair!

When I started riding the school bus, I used to sit on the back seat but was intimidated by the sixth form boys for stealing their territory. Then I sat upstairs on the school bus but was bullied off because I wasn't cool enough. I ended up sitting at the very front of the bus and, on regular occasions, would stand by the bag rack and talk to the bus driver as I didn't feel comfortable with the prospect of having to share my seat with another kid. It was safer to be alone. It was quite common for kids to put charms on their school bags, and I wanted to keep up. But any decorations I put on my school bag would get stolen within a week, so by sixth form, my mum ended up making me a custom bag and sewed on the embellishments!

The only reason I generally didn't mind going to school between years nine and eleven was because I had a boyfriend, Henry. We were in love, and he made me feel just that little bit safer. But I began to feel scared of what people thought of me. I was the weird freak who was good at maths and chess, after all. I used to pretend I wasn't smart just to try and fit in, but it never really worked. I had a photographic memory until I was sixteen years old. I did my homework on the bus on the way to school, and I got good grades because I was simply lucky.

Meanwhile, my dad had a few years where he was out of a job, so now and again, we'd get free school meals. Things at home were often on a tight budget, but we made do. At the time, I couldn't understand why I couldn't go on the French/German Exchanges or the posher school trips, but the truth was we just couldn't afford to.

I was always trying to get out of PE. I was so self-conscious because of the skin condition on my legs. I'd try and forge letters from my mum to get me out of it, but I got caught out, so I had to endure being mocked in the showers. Thankfully, the teachers didn't pay much attention to who had a proper shower and who didn't, so I would avoid them or run through them with half my clothes still on! Thankfully, I never had to do any physical education for GCSE and onwards.

In year seven, I remember being frustrated and angry. I'd been in the football team in year six at primary school, but when I started secondary school, I was told that I wasn't allowed to join the football team because it was for boys. My teacher suggested I start my own girls' team, but I wanted to play football with the boys, not the girls! All the girls I knew feared the ball coming anywhere near them and were encouraged to play netball instead. The same occurred for cricket and rugby—being told they were for boys. I, therefore, ended up losing my interest in sport completely.

It put me at a brief advantage (and therefore enjoyed it) in year eight for the girls' hockey class. I'd come from a football background, and I had shin pads—none of the other girls did! The bullies tried to get me with the hockey ball, but I deflected it back to them, so they got hit, and my shin pads protected me. Cross country was horrible. I was the kid a lap behind (with asthma), and although I wasn't that large, I was stuck with the largest kids at the back. Year nine brought the opportunity to play badminton, and I loved the idea of that because Henry had chosen it. I enjoyed my physical education lessons for one term. The same year I skipped school for a day because I'd been put in a group in drama with my bullies, and I was terrified. The next day they knew I'd faked being ill, and they called me all sorts of names for the rest of the week, generally making my life as miserable as they could.

Year nine was also the year I did my first Duke of Edinburgh Award (Bronze). It was great fun and taught us teamwork, but we were also grouped with people we didn't necessarily get along with. During the expeditions, I was thankfully placed in a group of five that included Henry, and we were all friends. It was on the assessed expedition that I had my first kiss! We were both nervous, it was pitch black, but it was also one of those tender but amazing moments you never forget. We did laugh too, and I wasn't particularly anxious for the parts where I was with friends. The following year we were supposed to do the Silver Award, but three friends dropped out, leaving just me and Henry. Henry was confident and had other friends he could join. I got anxious and dropped out, as I feared those people. They made me feel uneasy. I never got to do my Silver Award because of that. I think Henry went all the way and got his Gold Award, and I was always slightly jealous that he was more confident than me.

Year ten brought its own challenges. I tried to rebel against my parents. This started when I cut my hair because I was sick of my fringe. My fringe made me sweat more, which was just another thing for the bullies to notice. The previous year, I'd tried to clip it to the sides but was bullied for that, so this was the year I got rid of it completely. I was also fed up with being bullied about how I looked, so I rolled my school skirt up like the rest of my peers, and my tie gradually became shorter. My form tutor was strict and used to pull me up for my uniform, but this was the year I tried to answer back. This landed me in lunchtime detentions. It was a catch-22—be bullied or get in trouble with the tutor. The latter was preferable.

My years in sixth form were mainly distracted by boys, and most notably my first experience of a love triangle. I was barely paying attention in class, but thanks to my waning photographic memory, I just about got away with it. I had my friendship group, but I was still vulnerable to bullies. I had a really good friend who was the younger sister of one of my classmates. We used to attend cipher club together and enjoy cracking codes after school. We entered a national challenge that year, and we really got into it, until one day when she decided I was annoying and proceeded to slam my fingers in the school hall's piano while I was trying to play it! We never spoke again after that day.

Throughout my secondary school life, I was terrified of being seen as a grass, so I just took the bullying quietly but went home crying. As a teen, I spent a lot of time in my bedroom. I never really studied. Sometimes, I'd be writing my diary/journal, poetry, stories, and even music. I loved arts and crafts too, and particularly loved to crochet and make cards for people.

As far as friends went, I never had many, and I always seemed to be the third wheel. A set of best friends, and me. This happened throughout secondary school until sixth form. In sixth form, there were eight of us, but I always felt like a bit of an outcast because my ex was in there, and I was dating another guy by then. I only properly stayed in touch with very few from school. Regular contact—none.

LOVE TRIANGLES

Love triangles are such dangerous things. They're like Bermuda triangles, except you know where the corners are; you just don't understand what the hell is going on in the middle!

It happened twice in my life. The quiet one who was scared of everything—how? I guess I'll never know, but despite all of the bullying, I was always pretty good at holding down a boyfriend. I got my first boyfriend, Henry, when I was thirteen. I was such a failure, though. I was so naïve that I didn't realise if a boy asked you out, and you accepted, that meant you were an item—duh! So yeah, that first relationship could have easily lasted nearly four years, but we were four months into it, and a friend told me I was already dating him, and I hadn't realised. (Yes, I got mocked for that. That was my own stupid fault.) But the guy waited for me. We believed it was true love like you do when you're thirteen. I wrote in my journal that we'd get married at twenty-one and have kids at thirty. However, we spent all the time that we could together. He was a very friendly guy and would flirt unwittingly with other girls. In time I became clingy and insecure.

In year eight, I also met Jonesy by accident when we inadvertently took each other's bags home! (I was into football then, so my bag was a very boyish Umbro one.) Over the next few years, we became friends but had a love-hate relationship. He was also being bullied so we could relate to each other more.

I embarrassed myself in a spat with Jonesy on the school bus when I was about fifteen. I yelled to him, a bit louder than I thought I had, "AT LEAST I CAN GET A GIRLFRIEND!"

Cue awkward silence from the rest of the bus, then hysterical laughter from the sixth formers from the back as I turned beetroot red and muttered, "I meant boyfriend...obviously...," under my breath. That boy never let me live that one down.

By the time I was sixteen, and despite all the on/off fighting, I was falling in love with Jonesy, but I was still in love with Henry. Right through my GCSEs, all I could think about was those two boys, and I'd just got my first mobile phone too, so many texts went back and forth. Jonesy admitted he fancied me, and that threw me into complete turmoil.

I could have done so much better at my GCSEs, but life got in the way. I was both hyperactive and depressed, as well as anxious. I didn't want to hurt Henry. Why couldn't society let me date both of them? After playing endless loops of '*Too Much Love Will Kill You'* by Queen and writing into numerous diaries, I finished with Henry and started dating Jonesy, and that wasn't the end of it!

It was such a mess, and it's one of those things you don't forget. Sat on the floor of one of the computer rooms and kissing Henry again behind some cabinets. We still loved each other, but we had to part ways. That final kiss was savoured, and Jonesy never found out.

After that, Henry seemed to go off the rails a bit. He started partying and drinking, hanging out with the 'cool' guys. I felt left behind but was also happy with Jonesy. We had a real chemistry between us, but it was also very intense and purely emotional.

I used to skive psychology classes because that's when his music class was happening. I spent time in the music office with other sixth formers, mainly from the jazz band I was a part of. I'd even skive registration sometimes and pretend to have 'important' things to attend to. I hated my form class; it was full of bullies. I'd quite often be found behind the stage with Jonesy, as he operated the sound and lighting for assemblies, and I thought it was really cool!

I was still clingy, insecure and anxious. He was a lot more mature than me. He got a Saturday job when he was sixteen. I was finally allowed a paper round when I was seventeen. My parents couldn't afford for me to learn to drive, but he was learning when he turned seventeen and borrowed his mum's car, so he could pick me up, and we were able to go places. The downside was his mum was single, so she used to go everywhere with us.

The only time we were alone was when we went to a festival in the summer and pretended we had a tent each, which happened just once.

He was a year behind me at school, so when I was halfway through sixth form, he left school and joined the sixth form at a college across the other side of town. I was hurting, but I also understood he had to go there as he knew what he wanted to do as a career, while I had no idea. The distance grew again when I went to university two hours away. We survived, but only just, until he started university. He moved slightly closer, but the mental distance between us just grew. He found independence from his mum; he found a new set of friends. He moved on without me. I'll never forget feeling abandoned but being too scared to message him in case he was busy. He was always busy.

He was still in freshers' week at his university, and I had just moved into my student house. I was alone, and a massive spider ran across the floor in the dim light. I was absolutely terrified of spiders, and I had no one to call to come and rescue me as Jonesy was a couple of hours away. I messaged him and hopped straight on a train to see him. It was the only thing I could think of to escape the spider, as there was no way I could sleep in my house that night. Once I was on the train, the fear of the spider turned into excitement at seeing my boyfriend.

I was so excited that we'd get to spend time together!

When I got there, I spent a couple of days with him and his new flatmates. They had a party which I remember following them to, wanting to fit in but being anxious and not knowing what to say or do. I felt really uncomfortable and didn't fit in at all. They were all outgoing and full of energy. They were dressed for a night out, and there I was shuffling along nervously in jeans and a black top, but I smiled through it anyway. The next day he had lectures to go to, so I was left in the flat on my own. I was too shy to try and go out or talk to anyone, so I just sat and waited for him for most of the day. When he came back, we spent some time together, and it was almost bittersweet. I'd missed him so much, and little did I know it was the last time I'd officially see him. He walked me to the train station and waved off a very emotional girlfriend.

After being together, I realised that time is just a concept. My life was pretty empty, so time passed by monotonously and slowly. Jonesy was having the time of his life, working part-time, so time passed a lot quicker for him. One day I just decided to send that fateful message. I'd missed him, and he hadn't spoken to me for a few weeks. I was too scared to pick up the phone. I was too scared to message him in case he was busy. I ended up emotional and depressed. I left a message on his MSN, and he reckoned his flatmates saw it. It was an angry message. I was hurting! Within a day he phoned me. We were on the phone for an hour, but he basically told me he no longer loved me, and the friendship wasn't there anymore either. That was it. That was the end. I'd wasted three years with him. All those memories. What for?

'It is better to have loved and lost than never have loved at all!' - Moulin Rouge. That was my go-to film at the time.

I bumped into him that Christmas, and my heart was in my mouth; I hid. My mum was delivering Christmas cards and said hi to him and his mum, but I cowered in the car. That was the last I ever saw of him.

I was then single for eighteen months, and it was painful. It was the closest I'd ever been to full depression. I was suicidal at worst and nervous at best. I was too scared to talk to people, so sank fourteen hours a day into online gaming. It dulled the loneliness when I was on it, but it didn't help my confidence in real life either. My friend at university, Clare, looked out for me and tried to invite me to things. It was appreciated, but I was always very shy and nervous, so I would sit in corners and stare at the floor. She would check in on me, though, so those moments had conversation. I remember in my third year being invited to a lunch club. It gave me something to look forward to, and I was finally starting to come out of my shell.

It was the start of my master's degree when the next triangle happened. How can it happen twice in my life? I'd only had the first two boyfriends, and then the next came in two as well...ahhh! One guy jumped straight in, but I met them both in the same week. I was in quite a low place then, and I think I just accepted out of fear of being forever on my own, so Liam and I started dating. The more we got to know each other, the less we had in common. He even exclaimed he didn't like music—music was my life! He was also sending me mixed signals. I was still innocent then. I didn't initially believe in sex before marriage. I note here that with Jonesy, I'd decided to myself that if the moment felt right, I'd change my beliefs for him, but it never happened. This new guy said he respected my choices but then tried to pressure me into sex. I almost gave in, but at that weak point, I stopped myself and realised I was falling for the other guy.

Meanwhile, the other guy, Dr G, had taken a more tentative approach. He took the time to get to know me as a friend, and the more I got to know him, the more we found we had in common. At least this triangle was a no brainer. I had to finish with Liam to get with Dr G. I knew this guy was 'the one', though. I'd never been so sure of anything in my life.

But anxiety made me scared to finish with Liam, so although I did dump him face to face, I told some feeble excuse about having to distance myself to concentrate on my degree. Liam thought my parents had told me to dump him, but I didn't have the heart to tell him I'd already found my soulmate.

A mere three days later, I set up with the soulmate. It had never felt so right. Even though the first few months were a little rocky, we worked through everything in the first stage of the relationship, had seen all sides of each other and were, therefore, one hundred percent comfortable with each other. After five months together (convenience of student tenancy ending), I moved in with him and never looked back.

I've been married to my soulmate, Dr G, for just over nine years and together for over fourteen years. I got married at twenty-six and had a child at thirty-one. It may not have been to my first boyfriend, but the age predictions weren't too far off. Was this the first hint of goal setting, perhaps?

THE UNDERGRAD BIT

Why did I end up where I went? Because my brother told me it was a pretty place. Not because I actually wanted to go there. I wanted to go to York originally. Simply because I was that scared of leaving home. York was where a lot of family were, so I'd be safe. I'd made plans in my head to move in with one of my aunties where she could look after me. It sounds so ridiculous now, but it also is a good indicator of how anxious my mind was getting by then.

I didn't get the requirements for York, so I had to look at other options. I ended up with Bangor and Huddersfield. (Huddersfield because that's where my oldest friend, Tom, also a musician, was headed.)

2003 was the year we tried to go to as many university open days as were feasible. My dad was able to drive me to all of them, but the furthest and most memorable (for all the wrong reasons) one was Durham. I wish they could have asked for preferences because they put me in the sports college, which, as soon as I found out, instantly triggered me! I had no interest in sports, and naturally, those sports college students wanted to show the newcomers a good night out involving lots of drinking and partying. It was my worst nightmare, so once we were checked into our rooms, I stayed there—all night. With my headphones in, I listened to The Darkness 'Permission to Land' on loop! I got a few hours' sleep, and when my dad picked me up the following morning, I vowed never to go back there!

Bangor had a lower requirement to get in compared to York, so I went to the open day with my parents just to see what it was like, and ended up loving it, so I set my heart on it after that. Come September and getting ready to go, I had to say goodbye to Jonesy. I remember I'd packed all my clothes away, so all I had left was a baggy festival t-shirt, but my brother took some photos of us together, and I held on to them while we were together, as it was the closest I could get to him for a while.

In my first freshers' week, I was scared of everyone. My mum cried when she left me, and my dad just said I'll get used to it. I was homesick, but I was also determined to make it work, so I got on with stuff. I joined societies. I tried to go out to the pub crawls. Despite all that, I was too scared to strike up conversations or approach groups of people and introduce myself. A lot of the societies I signed up for, I never went to the events, I was too shy.

I did make it to badminton for the year and tried to get involved with the music society. A couple of people looked out for me, so I wasn't completely alone, and I survived. I'd have moments of confidence, but also was constantly being pushed in a certain direction right from my early years.

My parents wanted me to be a secondary school music teacher. I didn't know any different. I thought I was confident on piano, so did first study viola in order to get the free lessons, rather than pick my strongest instrument. That lesson hit me hard when I failed the performance module in first year, meaning I couldn't continue as a performer. I was also scared of the head of performance, who happened to be my personal tutor. When my gran died the night before my first performance exam, the sadness and the anxiety of an exam made me shaky and emotional. They heard me play and said, "We thought you had potential, but we were wrong." Those words have stuck in my head ever since and probably led to my major fear of judgement for being a performer in general. No encouragement or support was offered. That was it. I'd failed the module.

Included in my first-year memories was being humiliated by the 'Baroque' professor because it was invite-only, and he'd invited every string player in my year apart from me. Apparently, he didn't know I played the viola, despite it being my first study instrument.

I was so shaky for a certain module that when it came to a performance, with equally shaky flautist, Sophie, it became a vibrational duet for shaky harpsichord and flute! I joined the main orchestra but was ignored most weeks, which caused me to fade away and drop out, resulting from dirty looks every time the conductor saw me. He never once asked if I was ok or asked me *why* I left. Due to all my failings at performance, I moved over to composition. It was behind the scenes and a bit safer than putting myself out there. What I didn't bargain for was the criticism and lack of encouragement from various tutors. Arts is such a subjective field, and I was too naïve to realise until it was too late.

I'd always liked making Christmas cards for family and close friends at home, so I thought I'd make Christmas cards for the people I thought were my friends in the first year. When I barely got any back, I was devastated. I felt like I'd put the effort in for nothing, and no one cared. After that, I never sent a round of Christmas cards again and would generally wait for someone to send me one before sending one back.

My other nightmare was presentations. Any genre or composer module, a presentation was expected. I'd have the same reaction as I did for exams, but obviously, there was a whole class watching me for these. I'd cry at home, and by the time I arrived, I'd be a shaking wreck! If I read from a script, I got marked down even though everyone said to use prompt cards. If I used prompt cards and got a mental block (which happened most occasions), I'd be completely lost! The only time I got upwards of a C grade for a presentation was the one I forgot about until the morning of. I made it up as I went along, but because it was a subject I genuinely liked, 'The New vs. Old Dr Who' themes, I came across as more confident. A lesson I took with me several years later—you do better if you're confident and winging it!

I started second year slightly optimistic and signed up to be the music society's webmaster, with the idea that Jonesy would teach me how to build it. That was October.

We split up at the beginning of November. Due to splitting up with Jonesy in the first semester of second year, I basically spent my second year playing online PC games. I'd play up to fourteen hours a day, often forget to eat, go to bed at 5 am and get up at lunchtime. I thought no one cared about me, so why should I care about me? I remember just after the split, walking to the pier and contemplating jumping off the end. Ironically, my anxiety stopped me. I feared water, and I couldn't swim. *'Look at the beautiful sky. It's sunset. You'd miss that surely?'* I brought my thoughts back down to earth and just sat on a bench contemplating my pittance of a life.

That website I was supposed to be building never got off the ground. I remember attending meetings and every now again muttering that I'd sort it, but I never did because I didn't know how, and I was too scared to ask someone else for help. The rest of that year, I'd just about remember to do my coursework. I was so dozy one day I put the wrong cover sheets on my essays. (I had two similar modules run by the same lecturer, but he wasn't impressed.) Again, no tutors recognised that I was struggling, and I was too scared to ask for help. I only just scraped a pass in second year.

I had a crush on a guy in my second year too. Those eighteen months of singledom equated to a lot of unrequited love, where I'd admire them from a distance. At the end of my first year, there was Dom, who I used to watch playing badminton. Then second year was the Music Society Orchestral conductor, Ben. I fancied him a lot, but he never looked twice at me. I'd sometimes dream that he'd notice me and wake up sad that he still didn't know I existed.

The two friends that had really stuck by me in my first year, only one of them, Clare, was still around. Clare looked out for me. I remember going to the second-year annual dinner and being complimented on how slim I looked. What they didn't realise is that's what depression did to me. I basically starved myself for a few months by forgetting to eat because I was too immersed in my games, and all I wanted to do was play and sleep.

Third year hit, and I was just about starting to get out of my shell a little. Clare stuck by me and remembered to invite me to things, but I always felt inferior and like a tag-along. I tried to join in but ultimately would always be sat in a corner. At parties, it was usually by the food, so I could pretend to look busy. There was a guy who was similarly socially awkward, so in time we found each other and sat together, often moaning about our sad lives and how no one talked to us.

Clare was also chairperson of the society that year. She encouraged me to go for secretary, so I did. I really enjoyed that. I could sit in the corner and take notes at meetings, feeling vaguely important but also not having to say anything.

I was also briefly a DJ for the student radio station. I had a classical music show. A guy who was studying chemistry but also played the viola offered to help out, so I was glad of the assistance. There was one problem. I was more Classic FM, and he was more Radio 3. As the term went on, we ended up getting annoyed by each other. I'd had good feedback, but barely anyone listened to him. I had the first hour; he had the second. After that semester, he'd become the programme controller, so my show disappeared. I was miffed and thought it was because he wanted me out. I disappeared completely from the radio station then, too anxious to socialise because I was convinced that they didn't like me.

One memory that made me laugh during my time there was Ben, the conductor I had a crush on, was being interviewed for the upcoming concert! The other DJ interviewed him, and he boasted that he had such a wide music taste. "I love Bach right up to the Avant Garde!" I couldn't keep a straight face but stifled a laugh. Mate, that's not wide music taste. I like Death Metal and Vaughan Williams—that's wide! It was at that point I started to think maybe Ben was overrated. Later on, I found out that he had decided he was gay anyway, and people told me I'd had a lucky escape. He was self-obsessed and arrogant.

There was a housemate of mine in third year, Noah, that I also had a crush on. He played the guitar and would sometimes sing me Green Day songs. (They were my favourite band at the time.) I loved him to bits, but he was so unreliable. I'd get in a mood because he hadn't turned up to something or supported me in my presentation. I used to go and watch him and his band play at the local pub. He was completely oblivious about my crush for the whole time, and of course, I was too scared to say anything to him, so it stayed that way, and at the end of the academic year, he moved out, and we parted ways.

As far as academics went, that was going downhill too. I bucked up my ideas, but due to my interests (film and music), they assigned me a supervisor that wasn't even there! He'd recently left the university but was contactable only via phone. With my severe anxiety about phones, I mentioned to the admin that I thought I might need a different supervisor, but she sent me away saying it would be fine. It took me until the second semester to finally get the message across, so I was assigned to a different supervisor just one month before the final deadline. Even though it was a rushed project, I achieved mediocre marks and just enough to pass. Overall, I came out with a 2:1, which was enough to get on the master's course, but I knew my parents would have preferred it if I'd have got a first. For all the wrong reasons, the other most memorable module in my third year was conducting. I was a bumbling, anxious mess right up to the exam. I crashed out with a C grade, which in my parents' eyes, was a fail! Alas, the final semester of the final year was when I finally started to think I'd found some friends, but of course, a few months later, everyone graduated and went their separate ways.

I broke down that night of the last Spring Concert. Everyone was happy because they'd pulled off an awesome concert, and they all went to have a group photo together, except they forgot about me—everyone was in it except me. I was absolutely gutted. I took that to mean no one liked me, and no one cared. Clare realised and went looking for me, but I disappeared and hid in the practice rooms and sobbed Three friends left voice messages on my phone to apologise for leaving me out. Maybe they did care? I came back after an hour, and they were apologetic, but that memory, and the absence of a photo, spent many years haunting my mind.

The annual dinner was a bit better. I had people to talk to, I was included in the photo, but that occasion was there to mark the end of most peoples' chapters before they graduated. We had Facebook by then, so we kept in touch.

By that, I mean most of us added each other and then never spoke again.

Graduation was full of anxiety. The department had put on a social event so that all the music graduates and their parents could mingle. My parents just sat in a corner and didn't speak to anyone except for passing tutors, so I felt equally socially awkward. Because my friends were with their parents, I was too shy to approach them and missed out on so many photo opportunities just because the prospect of talking to anyone made me anxious!

EXCRUCIATING EXAMS

The exams I took at primary school were absolutely fine, and they were a walk in the park. The instrumental exams were a different story. My earliest memory of these was crying before going into violin exams and having to be calmed down by my teacher. I remember feeling sick to my stomach before piano exams and crying. My piano teacher was a lot more empathetic than any of my violin teachers ever were.

I was absolutely terrified of failing. Was it because my parents had forked out money for each exam, so it would have been a waste of their resources if I'd failed? This carried on from my junior years at primary school until I did my grade eight piano when I was seventeen. I never once got a distinction, but I'd occasionally get a merit. This was due to anxiety, but as a kid, I was told just to stop being silly and snap out of it.

I remember my violin teacher (a different one from the primary school one) when I was fourteen or so, suggesting

I take beta blockers for exams. My mum was horrified and told me I'd do no such thing, so I never found out what it was like to not be super anxious for exams. Ironically, I've been on beta blockers since I was twenty-eight due to high blood pressure.

Then there were the exams at school. My photographic memory came in very useful until GCSE level. I was actually not too bad at the exams, but I struggled to work in silence, and at home, I was always more productive when I had music on in the background. I'd get fidgety and watch every second of the clock until the exam finished and we were allowed to leave. My GCSEs didn't go too badly, although my best subject was graphic design. The exam was on my birthday, so I was too hyperactive that day and got an A instead of my predicted A* just because I couldn't concentrate! Henry got an A*, and rather than congratulate him, I felt jealous and that I'd failed, even though I'd still got an A. Overall, I did pretty well, so my parents rewarded me with the chance to get purple highlights in my hair and a portable minidisc player. That results day was an awesome day!

When AS/A2 levels hit, it was a whole different scenario. Somehow, I lost the photographic memory on which I'd relied so heavily in my younger years. I had to work twice as hard and revise for my exams for the first time. I was too scared to ask for help, so I used to copy bits from my friends and skip classes often. I was in the middle of a love triangle with Henry and Jonesy, so my concentration was far from studying.

When AS exams happened, the maths exam was on my birthday. You guessed it. I was too hyperactive again. I didn't do too well on that exam, so much so that my mum said I would have to re-sit it. Yet there was a compromise. I wouldn't have to re-sit it, as long as I promised to attend private tutoring classes with my uncle, who was a mathematician. For most of the following year, every time we visited those relatives, I'd have to attend an evening "class" while my aunt watched soaps in the background. I barely paid attention, and it was so dull, but I was diligent and pushed through somehow.

My A2 Levels didn't quite go to plan, and I ended up with B-C-C-D. Not one hint of an A. My mum just took one look at me on results day and said, "I hope you're going to re-sit those!" Hang on a minute. I'd been accepted to Bangor. Why should I re-sit when I'd been accepted? I declined her suggestion and took my results, accepting my place on the course at Bangor. My parents seemed to see my results as a failure, as in contrast to the gifts from my GCSE achievements, I received absolutely nothing that year.

Onwards to university. Music was handy, hardly any exams. The only exams I had to consider in first year were the performance module and a single genre study. I sadly never made it past the first year of performance.

The other first-year exam I had was Music Cultures of the World, and I didn't have a clue what I was doing. I found out you could leave the exam after thirty minutes, so I wrote my name, maybe a sentence and walked out of the exam. The silence disturbed me, and I hated it. Thankfully, I still passed the module because the coursework was passable.

When I was picking my modules for second year, I chose all the modules that didn't have exams and attempted to do the same for third year. There were a multitude of presentations to survive, but that was slightly less evil than the prospect of sitting an exam.

In third year, there was one final exam—conducting. It was my worst nightmare, and because I'd been anxious throughout the whole module, the exam was just a culmination of all the anxiety in one big mess. The exam was just fifteen minutes long, and I had to choose to conduct a choir or orchestra. We decided during the term, and I only chose choir because it was likely to be a smaller group of people compared to an orchestra. With a choir full of music students, they were going to be fairly good at singing, and I was so anxious I didn't know what to do or which piece to pick for my exam. The lecturer's assistant helped the students who needed it, and he chose a John Rutter piece for me. I didn't realise until several years later that John Rutter's choral pieces are not only very tuneful and harmonious but also very simple for a choir to learn. So, my worst nightmare was confirmed when I conducted the choir, and they sang it perfectly on the first attempt. The point of a rehearsal was to practice a piece that needed work. After the first sing-through, I was lost. My eyes wildly darted around. '*What the hell am I supposed to do next?!*' The tutor informed me I had twelve minutes left. I panicked. I asked them to sing it again and then tried to make some rehearsal points up, whilst going gradually redder and wishing the ground would swallow me up. I didn't do very well on that exam. I was awarded a C. In my (and my parents') eyes, I failed the module. But at least I got my degree. I was safe. I'd done it.

Fast forward a few years and I was learning Welsh. I hadn't forgotten about the issues of silence in an exam, but I was determined to learn Welsh properly. The first mention of an exam and my brain went into meltdown. I had to go into the corridor with the tutor and ask for help, and I also felt the need to explain why I burst into tears! That was the moment, though.

I finally asked for help!

There were two exams I remember sitting for Welsh, and both times I had a separate room to myself. The experience of sitting an exam was instantly improved. However, the first one I sat, I was praying that it wouldn't be in silence, so I ended up doing it to the 'soundtrack' of a manoeuvring lorry outside my window! I got a distinction for that one somehow. In the second exam, a couple of years later, I was even confident, and the speaking section was easier because we talked about music. The tutor conducting the exam happened to be a pianist too; I was at home.

That was the last time I ever did an exam. I at least know now that I *can* ask for help. It makes so much difference knowing what my options are and that it is possible to be supported properly.

TO BE DR & DR OR NOT TO BE

Towards the end of my first semester of third year, I had to start thinking about my future options. I was depressed and single. I didn't have a clue what I wanted to do but had my parents in the background adamant that I should do a Postgraduate Certificate in Education (PGCE). They were so pushy that during the Christmas break, one of my mum's colleagues spoke to me on the phone about all the benefits and rewards I could get if I did a PGCE. By the end of the phone call, I was coming to terms with the idea of doing a primary PGCE, but what I didn't realise was that the deadline for applications had already passed. Back to square one. It looked like a secondary PGCE was the only option.

Just before the Easter break, I'd applied for the PGCE and the opportunity for masters' degrees was highlighted during a lecture. Being terrified of change, and similar to the idea of staying on at the school sixth form, I saw the master's degree as a chance to essentially resist change. I ended up applying for both, much to my parents' distaste.

They said if I did the master's degree, I was on my own. I got accepted for both, even though I had to endure an interview for the PGCE and was pretty sure I'd destroyed my chances by actually talking too much! It was decision time. Do I dare defy my parents?

I honestly can't remember what triggered me to make the decision, but I went with my gut instincts and accepted the place on the master's degree course. A master's degree in composition, that's all I was really qualified for. It seemed like the easy option; no performing, no exams, just lots of coursework, essays and compositions. Two years part-time so I could pay for it myself. Perfect.

I got a job at the local supermarket as a checkout girl. Monotonous work, but it paid the bills. The rest of the team always lived for the weekend and wanted to get drunk, so naturally, I didn't fit in. My anxiety was quite high then. My 'stuck in corner, staring at floor' mode was going nowhere, and people had to come to me if they wanted to talk to me because I'd never go to them.

In September, just as I started my master's degree, I met the two guys I spoke of earlier, Liam and Dr G. The first semester went downhill, but the second semester got better. My anxiety was still sky high, and Liam had thrown me into emotional turmoil on a few occasions. I'd started staying up too late again and missing morning lectures.

By the time I got with Dr G, who was studying for a PhD, he offered me his office as my safe space, so I could get some work done without distractions. This was a lifesaver and probably made the difference between failing or passing my degree. My tutor offered no encouragement and had simply said I was going to fail. Thankfully for the second part, I had a different tutor who tried to help me, but ultimately, composition is an art. Art is very subjective. As a result, I never composed again after that master's degree. Doing the master's degree made me resent the very thing I became qualified in.

Studying for my actual master's degree was incredibly stressful. Due to a combination of not being able to ask for help and tutors who criticised but never encouraged, I was a mess mentally.

I never set foot in the library. I had the advantage that my parents hoarded books, so I had my own mini library in my room. It saw me through my undergraduate degree, but it was sometimes lacking for my postgraduate degree. I was too anxious to ask for help in the library, so I muddled through by myself, often not finding the resources I needed, desperately searching on the internet in the hope of finding something.

There was a particular module where I was the only student, so I used to have my lectures in his office. This always made me nervous, and the actual work I was assigned did nothing to improve that. I was once given an essay where I couldn't find any books, was given a bibliography entirely in Welsh and was too scared to ask for help in case the tutor thought I was a failure. There was a separate essay for the same module where I had to start it again because I hadn't understood the question properly.

The end of the master's degree saw me printing out my final project on my own printer as I was too anxious to try and use the university printers because if anything went wrong, I might have to speak to someone and ask for help. Towards the end of that course, I did wonder why I'd done it all. It seemed to be for nothing. But on reflection, if I hadn't have done the master's degree, I'd have never met my soulmate.

We graduated a year apart. My graduation was in the summer of 2010. I remember being anxious again but managing to get pictures with a couple of friends, the only friends I talked to for the whole day. I'd just got engaged the week before but didn't have an engagement ring to show. Dr G went AWOL when we were trying to take photos, so it was like he was imaginary as far as the friends were concerned. I later found out that he'd gone in pursuit of free food. He was a member of staff, so he'd been stewarding at the ceremony. I didn't attend the department event that time because of what happened at the first graduation.

Dr G's graduation was in 2011. It was all very posh because he was graduating with a PhD and was now officially Dr G! I attended his department event with him and his parents. I tried my best to be confident, but I found myself stuck in my seat, unable to talk to anyone unless they spoke to me! I was able to get into the ceremony because his colleague was working as a steward, so I sat high up on the balcony and kept to myself. I was proud of Dr G, but I also didn't have anyone to talk to. In a room full of strangers, I'd always make myself invisible.

It was around that year, whilst working as a note taker, that I considered doing a PhD myself. I'd have absolutely loved to have been a doctor. I was inspired by note-taking in some film modules and loved the idea of doing a PhD in film music. I was given the channels to enquire through, but ultimately my anxiety scared me off. Too scared to make any phone calls or email unknown people. Too scared to ask for help! In the end, I decided that just wanting to be 'Dr & Dr' wasn't enough to warrant doing eight years of a self-funded PhD.

We became Dr & Mrs the year after. It was great! He may have been a doctor of maths, but it made him look important, so whenever we booked hotels, the staff would always be super polite.

MUSIC WAS ALWAYS MY PASSION

Music is my life. It's now my passion. It wasn't always like that, though. So, where did it start? I don't actually remember that far back. My earliest memory was playing my mum's wooden recorder at the age of three on the floor at the back of the living room using an Early Learning Centre book. It had a picture of a boy in green on the front. Apparently, I could do quite a lot of things when I was three. My dad used to tell everyone I was doing a three-hundred-piece jigsaw at that age, whereas my own three-year-old was busy stuffing jigsaw pieces in places I'd never thought of.

When I went to school, it was straight in with the recorder, and I started playing the violin at the age of four. My mum insisted that was the instrument I chose. My recollection was somewhat different, though. I remember being told no to the drums, trumpet and saxophone. They were all too noisy.

As it turned out, I seemed to have perfect pitch, and with music being seen as a language, I took to the violin naturally. I was called talented from an early age. My violin teacher at primary school was often abrupt and wasn't very inspiring. I was too young to know any different, and when I cried at my exams, it was just assumed normal.

Before I started official lessons on piano, I was already learning through a programme on my dad's computer called *The Miracle*. It used a midi half-size keyboard to interact with, and it was fantastic fun. I must have been five or six years old at the time. I loved that you could play tunes along to the backing tracks, and essentially, I think the idea was to fill a jukebox, or you could get inspiration from it. It was great fun, and I loved playing it when I came home from school.

I also sang in choirs pretty much all the way through my childhood. I began with my local church choir at primary school, junior choir at secondary school, senior choir, chamber choir during sixth form, and finally the music society choir at university. My life growing up in choirs only really ended in 2016 when I became the accompanist to the music society choir. I was originally a soprano but ended up singing the alto parts. When I was thirteen and started dating Henry, he was a choirboy. When his voice broke, he ended up singing the lower part. Junior choir was a two-part choir, and I followed him. I still love singing in choirs but never had the confidence to sing solo except for one occasion where a friend dared me in 2007, and I squeaked anxiously, only to be told my voice was too weak. I never tried to sing solo again until 2021 in my Facebook community.

I started piano lessons when I was seven. Compared to my violin lesson experience, this teacher had a quieter personality, and she was a lot more patient and kinder. The stark contrast between the two instruments was clearly evident. I had four different violin teachers, but the same piano teacher all the way through. The conclusion by the end of my childhood was that I had lost interest in the violin but found my passion for the piano.

My experience with piano lessons was straightforward and I had lessons until I left for university. My teacher was lovely, looked after me, and stayed in touch with my mum after I'd left. I still hated practising, but I generally enjoyed my lessons. Later in life, when I was talking to my old piano teacher, she revealed she knew that I never properly practised, but she played along with it anyway. Since I had perfect pitch and was good at sight-reading, I thought I'd gotten away with it!

As a sixth-former, I joined the school swing band and learnt about jazz. I was the pianist and I loved it, but I was always nervous, and the prospect of having microphones in my piano freaked me out. I never once got to play a solo perfectly, which would result in me going red every time I made a mistake. It didn't help that in the band were both Henry (now the ex) and Jonesy, but I loved it, and I loved being part of it. They were some of my best school memories.

Towards the end of sixth form, I had the opportunity to play solo piano for a couple of concerts. The composer, Einaudi, was quite new on the scene then, so everyone wanted to hear his music. The first time I played 'I Giorni' was at a church with the chamber choir I was part of. I tried to play it from memory and ended up in an endless loop but somehow survived. The second piece I did was at the final Easter concert. Again, I survived, but I was shaking so much that the pedal was vibrating weirdly. It didn't help my nerves, it just made them worse. I was too shy to play in public right up until 2016, when I started to play in the local National Trust venue as a background artist.

With violin, the problem was that when you have multiple teachers, they each have their own teaching technique. With every violin teacher I had, I had to relearn all the techniques again, and it wore me down. It was boring. I was fed up, and I hated practising. I was proud I'd managed to achieve my grade five violin at the age of eleven, but I never went beyond that. At the start of secondary school was a teacher who left for London after a term, so the third teacher was the one I was supposed to settle with. I was around twelve or thirteen at the time. We had to change technique again. She'd bring out nail clippers and make me cut my nails in the lesson. She smoked in the lesson too. I had asthma, yet I was too afraid to report her for fear of her being angry at me. She also told me that she'd fallen out with the examination board ABRSM, so she wouldn't enter any of her students for their exams. I got nowhere between the ages of thirteen and sixteen.

Meanwhile, at school, I was roped into string group. I was one of a very small minority that could play in tune. I think there were three of us at peak. Every concert was just painful, but when I was in year nine, the teacher in charge used to guilt trip me into participating and even threatened to stop me from going on the annual school trip to Alton Towers if I didn't take part. Being forced into something like that was torture. When I got to sixth form, a different music teacher who was a cellist suggested setting up a string quartet. Phew, a chance to escape the din and make some proper music! I loved the string quartet—four competent musicians, with me on viola. My favourite memory was doing a concert with one of the other students playing the piano for a 'Piano Concerto' by Shostakovich. It was beautiful.

Outside of school, from the age of about nine or ten, I joined a local youth orchestra, and I did generally enjoy that, even though it was in the evenings, and I was usually really tired by then. In my mid-teens, I'd often be so tired I'd feel like I was nodding off. It was a club I wanted to be part of, despite the tiredness. I had a couple of friends there, even though I was generally too shy to approach new people. I'd usually hang around the sweets table during the break and sometimes people would talk to me.

We used to perform concerts every term, and I'd be nervous on the stage. We were lucky, for a few years we got to play our Christmas concerts at the Bridgewater Hall in central Manchester. We were even recorded by Greater Manchester Radio one year. I'd always be excited about the concert but nervous when playing or walking on and off stage.

In my mid-teens, it became apparent that my dad quite fancied me as the next Vanessa Mae, so I saved up money to buy an electric violin that I didn't really want. However, I couldn't say no and it did look fancy. I kept it for several years but never got to grips with it. It was shiny and white. I would have been one of the cool kids if I'd mastered it, but that never happened.

At the age of sixteen, I felt like my violin teacher decided I was a lost cause. I couldn't get to grips with the technique of vibrato, as the first teacher had never taught me how to do it, and this teacher assumed that I should have picked it up earlier on. She tried to teach me, but I just wasn't able to do it properly, so she suggested I switch to viola instead because it was easier. I jumped at the chance because it was different. Everyone played the violin, but no one played the viola. I managed to get away with a feeble attempt at vibrato. We ended up spending a few years playing challenging pieces, and then I left to go to university.

In the summer, just before my freshers' year at university, my youth orchestra went to the Netherlands on tour for a week. That was my first journey via air, and I was terrified. I also cried at the airport in front of everyone because, in a last-minute panic, I'd packed my manicure kit in my hand luggage and was mortified when it got confiscated. Despite the initial stress, the holiday itself was incredible. I was the only viola player, and I was playing to strangers. I was almost confident, and I kept a diary of my time there, which I treasure to this day. However, the experience at the airport was never forgotten, and I'm still afraid of airports and aeroplanes.

Things were going as well as they could for an anxious teenager until it was time to go to university. This is where things went wrong. I tried to be "clever". I had two instruments under my belt, but at university, I was only entitled to one set of free lessons. I figured I'd pick my weaker instrument because I needed the lessons, not the stronger instrument because I wanted to do well at my degree. I only realised my error of judgement when I failed

Performance in first year. To make matters worse, I'd actually borrowed my teacher's viola, and she died halfway through my first year, so I had to give it back as per her will and borrow the generic university owned one instead.

My gran died the night before an exam at the end of my first semester. I was too shy to ask for support or tell the tutors what had happened, so I just got on with it and consequently failed the module. I sucked it up and just assumed it was because I was rubbish. The tutor assessing it said, "We thought you had potential, but we were wrong!" Well, that was my tiny bit of performance confidence well and truly shot! I did composition for the rest of my education.

I went away from playing completely, not getting my own keyboard until 2008. I stuck around the music department on and off until 2019, supporting various students and finally being a sighted assistant to a visually impaired student. Around 2014, I decided I didn't want to be a musician anymore and got an office job. My parents were very disappointed; there was no hiding it. I did someone's maternity cover for a year and convinced myself the office was the way forward. However, as 2015 went sour, I found myself missing my music. Due to us moving house at the end of that year, I finally had space to get my piano back. My dad offered me my childhood piano at that point, so we arranged to get it transported to Anglesey. It arrived in my new house, and Dr G told me he'd support me if I wanted to try and go freelance.

January 2016 was when I decided to go self-employed as a piano teacher. At that point, it was because I felt I had nothing left. I was only good at one thing—playing the piano. I had nothing left to lose.

A LIFE OF EMPLOYMENT

An anxious person who's terrified of change and new things, what could possibly go wrong? I didn't want to leave school because of change. I made it to university. Then I was too scared to leave university because of change. That's not where it all started, though.

Most kids got a paper round at thirteen, but my parents wouldn't allow me to. We went to see the grandparents every other weekend, so I had duties which meant I couldn't get any regular job, even when I hit sixteen, and all my friends got Saturday jobs. When I was seventeen, I was allowed to get a paper round. My brother was thirteen at that point, so of course, he was allowed at the same time. We used to share the neighbourhood and be out at the crack of dawn. It was all fine until I got chased down the road by a gang of cats at seven o'clock on a Saturday morning, which terrified me so much my brother had to finish that bit of my paper round!

I still had the paper round just before I left for university, but my dad took it over as he was an early riser and was unemployed at that point.

At university, I didn't need to get a job. However, I attempted to volunteer at the local health food shop and enjoyed being paid in smoothies. I was too scared to ask any questions, and I struggled to get up early enough, so I just 'disappeared' and then avoided the shop and any eye contact. Anxiety had won again.

I was fine financially, though. In fact, by the end of my first year, I'd saved a thousand pounds from my student grants and loans, which I later put towards doing my master's degree. My mum believed I should be productive during the summer holidays, so she put me in contact with the head office of an exam board at the end of my first year. That was my summer job whilst I was a student, and I did that two summers in a row.

The first year I did the summer job involved a thirty-minute walk, a thirty-minute train journey, and a forty-five-minute walk each way. It was a hell of a commute! '*Was this what I was supposed to expect in the real world?*' I thought to myself.

When my dad had a job, he'd usually be out of the house before sunrise and not be back until after tea. Eventually, I found out a guy, who was working there at the same time, lived up the road from me and could drive, so he offered me a lift and that saved time. Like with most friends, we got along great, but we never stayed in touch. I was simply too anxious to phone or message him once the job was over.

The second year was a completely different experience from the first. I ended up in the basement, where I wanted to be because they were allowed to have the radio on. I became friends with the basement crew. Henry was also working in the offices but in a different department. Two major things happened that year:

I was single and I thought I still loved Henry. I was encouraged by my oldest friend, Tom, to tell him, so I plucked up the courage when we had a party around his house, and his reply was "Awww!" with a very patronising pat on the head and then nothing else was said. I was mortified! The next day he was flirting with another girl, and I saw them kissing. That was awkward, and I just wanted the ground to swallow me up.

The other major thing that year was a girl who lived down the road also had a job there. Her mum was good friends with our neighbour, so the neighbour suggested she give me a lift. This was a mistake and a half. I remember catching her red-handed standing outside the building where we worked, telling everyone how much of a sad little geek I was. She didn't know I was standing behind her. She went quiet, but she never apologised. We drove home in silence. I was shaking with humiliation and anger. We were four miles from home, and it was raining. I don't remember what was said, but we started arguing, so I waited until she stopped at a red light, got out of the car and said I would walk home. I did it to prove I wasn't a pushover. I never paid her that bit of petrol money. We never spoke to or saw each other again. I felt triumphant at that moment that I'd stood up to someone. However, it took me several weeks to sort out my head after that incident.

I didn't go back there the following year because I got a job as a checkout girl at the local supermarket where I went to university. They asked me about pre-booked holidays. Traditionally, I'd never work on my birthday. I was called over the speaker on my birthday and the other checkout people found it funny, but I was just upset that they'd asked me to state my dates and then obviously not paid any attention. I only learnt about it because one of my colleagues messaged me to tell me.

I lasted eighteen months in that job. I'd get disciplinaries when I didn't sell any saver stamps. I'd get told off for my attitude. I dropped an apple once and the woman complained to the manager that I'd thrown it at her! I got a disciplinary once for not opening bags for customers; my dry hands meant I couldn't open them quick enough.

Christmas time caused even more drama. My parents stressed me out when I was at home, but I also got homesick easily. Being told I couldn't go home for Christmas, I had a meltdown in the middle of the supermarket. My colleagues felt sorry for me, but I felt so small and stupid, knowing customers saw me in that state too. It didn't happen just once either. It happened on both Christmases when I was working there.

It was the following February when I handed in my notice. I'd been dating Dr G for just over a year by then, and he was a note taker, so we worked out the maths that I could earn more as a note taker, working fewer hours than I was doing as a checkout girl. I handed in my notice and left a week later. The timing of this happened to be a week after they threatened to sack me for not opening bags 'correctly'. The best feeling! They were short-staffed, and I landed them in it; that was a win in my book. When asked why I left on any future job applications, I would always put 'it served its purpose'.

For the next few years, I was a note taker. I took notes for less able students in various subjects. By the end of it, I had eight unofficial degrees across history, music, social work, theology, and computer science! In my head, being a note taker meant I never had to leave the university. Shame it was a low paid zero-hours contract. I also volunteered at the local health food shop again. The same health food shop I'd volunteered at and disappeared from in my first year at university. I found a tiny bit of confidence, and I helped them out for over a year.

As far as life itself went, I was just grateful I didn't have to make any major life changes. Both Dr G and I were note takers. That's how we'd met. We were the first and only note taker romance! In 2009, he became the note taking coordinator, so when talking about previous jobs, it's true that the only manager I've never fallen out with was the one that became my husband.

The assumption here was that he'd give me preferential treatment, but it was, in fact, the opposite. I was his short-notice cover when needed —no advantages at all. I was so paranoid about being judged that when I married him in 2012, I kept my maiden name just for that job. I was so good at being professional that people didn't even know we were together, let alone married. It was almost funny if it wasn't sad. I saw it as a kind of game after a while, to see just how professional I could be.

In between note taking, I did other jobs to supplement the small income. For a few years, I was an exam assistant. The job description was a bag guard. (Where I got to play my Nintendo DS quietly outside the exam room.) Then I got promoted to being the person on duty outside the sick bay. That was a lot more interesting, as I got to whisper to people outside the exam room and get to know the other members of staff a bit. I even saved the day once when I realised the written music exam had arrived without any manuscript paper.

I also got to scribe for actual exams, as well as invigilate. I did that up to 2019. It was an interesting experience but didn't really help my low income levels. I often ended up with a purple knuckle at the scribe job, with the record exam having to handwrite thirty A4 pages in three hours! The invigilating was the only real time I read books. I'd usually pop to the local library just before exam season and borrow a handful of books to last me through the job.

In 2011, I was a sighted guide for a guy called Miles. This wasn't great because it was a constant battle for him against the courses, the tutors and everything else. Things just weren't accessible. I once had to sit in a meeting with a disability contact and the disability manager, being accused of not doing my job properly, despite the fact that the job description didn't say it was my responsibility to make sure things were accessible. As far as I was concerned, I was being paid peanuts; it wasn't in my remit.

I was angry but too anxious to fight back and stand up for him and myself. We just took it on the chin and got on with it. It was that May I got diagnosed with high blood pressure. That was the same summer I got married. When

I was working with my students, I would give them my all. I liked to create a good rapport. I liked to be known as trustworthy and reliable. I was indeed, but then I was accused of not doing my job properly or lacking initiative. It was the May exam period and Miles was asking me for help. It was stressful, but we survived, though the resources should have been accessible in the first place.

Sadly, he didn't quite pass the year, so he had to do the extra projects in the August. August was the month I got married. The week before my wedding, I said to myself I wouldn't help him past a certain point.

The Friday before my Sunday wedding, I was due to go to my venue when he messaged me. He was expecting me to help him with his projects. I'd let it go that long, but I couldn't cope. I was literally on the way to my wedding. I handed responsibility over to the school's administrator. This was the first time I said no and put some boundaries up. Until then, I wouldn't ever say no. I was often walked all over and taken advantage of just because I couldn't say no.

Every summer, I would be effectively jobless—no hours and plenty of time. I usually spent it playing video games, or there was the summer when we had to live at Dr G's parents' house, and I had nothing to do other than go to the gym or play my Nintendo 3DS. I got an office job for a couple of years, but when it went sour, I went back to what I knew and was a note taker again for the rest of the academic year. It was easy going this time. I'd just go to lectures, take notes, hand them over.

Although I set up as a piano teacher in early 2016, I still

had the zero-hours contract on the side and became a sighted guide again in the September. This time it was a student called Michael. Four years between them, you'd think things would be more accessible. Nope! This student also faced battles every day, but this time it was the disability services that picked up the slack like it should have been the first time.

That freshers' week was when I found out I was pregnant, so my student went on the whole 'journey' with me. I didn't just create a rapport, we became good friends too. He struggled through and barely passed first year. There were just so many obstacles and most of them were out of our control. I really wanted to see him through to the end of his year, but my baby came three weeks early, so I had to miss his last week of the term. I had to hand him over to another support worker. I later found out that didn't go so well, and even though I couldn't have done anything about it, I couldn't help but feel partially responsible.

For Michael's second year, I was there, but I wasn't there. I turned up when I was needed, but most of the time, I was a zombie. There were supposed to be two of us working with him, but he didn't get along with the other person, and apparently, they weren't trained properly either. By the May of second year, he nearly dropped out of university altogether, and I found myself apologising to him and his parents for not being there for him when we went for lunch together at the end of the year. I promised them that we'd make it work in the third year.

We started third year with fire in our bellies! We knew what we wanted, and he knew how to fight. We quickly realised that I wasn't allowed to be his mentor, so they forced another person on him instead. She was trying to be helpful but was essentially useless. She didn't know him, and he was more capable than she was. That first semester was a war! I had that bit of fire, and I took it to my manager. She reduced me to tears because she accused me of crossing boundaries and not being professional. I'd built a relationship with Michael, and he knew he could trust and rely on me. I was devastated. However, there was a silver lining. His mum contacted me after that meeting and offered me a private contract instead. Screw the establishment. Michael knew what he wanted. We made it work for the rest of the year, and he celebrated his successful graduation that summer.

In 2019, the same summer of Michael's graduation, the manager I'd fallen out with earlier in the year informed me that they wouldn't be renewing my contract with the university. I simply replied with, 'I was expecting that, and I'm ready to go alone as a self-employed person, so I guess everyone's happy. Best Wishes'.

Never again will I work a zero-hour contract because I'm afraid of change—I'm worth more than that. In 2014, I got an office job. I believed that's what I was meant to do because that's what society expected me to do. The call of a full salary was far too appealing when I'd been making virtually nothing since I'd graduated. It was maternity cover in the university. I don't know how I got the job, but I managed to ace an interview for once at The Housing Office. Exciting!

Then ensued a year of me trying to do my best and making a name for myself as the one that gets stuff done.

I always felt inferior, though, and I never fitted in. I knew the colleagues before I started as it was the same department that Dr G worked in. It was an office full of women, but I was at least fifteen years younger than the next youngest person. They liked to go drinking at the weekends. I didn't drink. With my severe social anxiety, every time I went out for an occasion, I'd struggle to make conversations. Looking back at photos, I could barely smile as I was simply uncomfortable. I constantly tried my best to fit in, and it was draining. I actually really loved the job; it was varied, I got to meet lots of people, and being an official member of staff meant I could book free venues myself.

When it was due to end, the last month of the job was filled with job interviews all over the university, as I grasped at straws in an attempt to keep within the staff role. This was seen in my mind as the safe option because if I stayed within the university, I wouldn't have to change too much. The exercise was futile though; I failed every single interview, and every time I failed, it was for a different reason.

"You were too nervous."
"You weren't qualified enough."
"You didn't know enough."
"Someone else was better suited."

However, the week before I was due to leave, I had one last interview. Event planning, my forté! I was confident about this one. I was so confident, in fact, that I forgot to talk about the job I was applying for. I crashed out of the university. I think this was my first experience of burnout.

I'd completely worn myself out, I was stressed, I was feeling useless. I vomited all over the toilet at home.

A week later, a local private student housing company was looking for an administration assistant. I applied for it but had already resigned that I failed at job interviews and stopped caring. Ironically, my 'not caring' attitude got me the job. Before I started, they contacted me to ask if I'd consider being the assistant manager as they were impressed by my interview, and there was a vacancy higher up. I accepted it and told myself a challenge was good. It was also the first and last time I'd actually declared my anxiety disorder in a job application. Accepting that job was probably the worst mistake I'd ever made. However, at this point, Dr G decided to sell our house and move up the property ladder. Like the last job, I tried my best. I just wanted to fit in.

I wasn't trained properly, then was criticised for not asking enough questions. I was given the worst jobs on my first day, chasing debts from people who owed money. I was forced to get over some of my fears pretty quickly: using the lift, using the phone, talking to unknown people, travelling to English cities for training, even using the train.

I lasted three very rocky months on probation. I like to try and work things out myself, and I'm usually a quick learner and don't need to ask questions as I'm quite good at finding solutions myself. One month into the job, the site manager went on holiday, leaving me in charge. I had a meltdown on the first day about how he hadn't trained me properly. One of my colleagues reported me to the regional manager, and before I knew it, he was paying us a visit and asking me what was wrong. When the site manager returned, he heard about everything I'd said and decided I just didn't like him rather than sort out the training that was missing. I struggled on for another month and a half. Just before I went on holiday myself, the site manager extended my probation because I didn't ask enough questions. I spent that holiday with my friends ranting and venting about my job, to the point my friends just sat me down and said, "Jen, you obviously need to resign!"

First day back on the job and I handed in my notice. I had to work my two weeks then I was free. That final week was almost enjoyable. I helped out some students, and I saved a delivery guy's keys from getting flushed down a drain. It was generally a feel-good week. I even had a proposal from a mature student and an offer to go to his party on the top floor of 'F' block. Apart from the fact I was already married, the idea of a party triggered me straight away, so I politely declined the party as well as the proposal.

The day before I was due to leave, the site manager walked out! The regional manager had just changed over, and he didn't like her, so he just upped and left. She came over to our site in person and managed to persuade me to stick around, but she also made the administration assistant into an assistant manager. Two assistant managers and no actual manager was always going to be risky, and it got out of hand very quickly.

Paul, who had recently graduated, was very arrogant and was a bit of a bully. He triggered my anxiety regularly and blamed me for anything bad that happened. He thought I was a loser because I was a gamer too. This onslaught lasted about two weeks until it all came to a head on the final day. I'd arranged a little event in the common room. We were able to have free pizza and some games. I'd invited some of my community along to boost the numbers. The other assistant manager began to stress and declared an emergency on the building even though the warning button had been flashing for the week before. My friend Ross was driving and wanted access to the car park, so his passenger rang me from the gate. It was a one-way street, so he was blocking the road. Paul was getting angry and shouted, "Don't let him in. We have an emergency to deal with!" I wanted to unblock the road, so I ran down, let Ross's car in and ran back. Paul flipped at me and started yelling at me in front of everyone. He told me he thought I was crap at my job, I didn't take it seriously, and I didn't care about the students. He told me I had no life and needed to get one and then told me to fuck off! I was already in tears by that point. I literally 'effed off' into the basement, sobbing.

Thankfully because my friends were there, they looked after me, and we eventually escaped through the basement and left the building. Paul was messaging me saying I'd left my computer on, but I never replied. We went to a pub at the other end of town, and then when it was dark, they drove me back to the office. I switched off my computer and emptied my desk drawers. I was never going to set foot in there again.

A couple of weeks later, I bumped into Paul in the local supermarket. I froze in fear as my heart leapt into my mouth. It took me several months to get over that experience. I was ashamed that I'd let a guy get to me so badly. I felt like I was a complete failure. I made sure I posted the office keys through the letterbox when I knew he'd be out. After that experience, I swore to myself that I would never have an office job or work in a private sector office ever again. That was September 2015, and I became self-employed in February 2016, after coming back from another burnout due to the bullying.

It was the end of 2015, and we had just moved house into our forever home. My last house had a study, but the difference this time was that my study was downstairs. It was roughly the same time my parents decided to get rid of the family piano, and my dad gave me a choice. Either he would sort it to get moved to my house, or he got rid of it completely. It held a lot of sentimental value to me, and I didn't want to see it go, so I accepted his offer to move it to my house. Over Christmas, I'd talked to Dr G a lot and knew I needed to sort out what I was going to do in the longer term.

After I'd walked out of my job from the office, I had fallen back into my safe job as a note taker. It was still very low income and zero-hours contracts, but at least I wasn't completely jobless either. Over the Christmas break, Dr G heard about the piano situation and suggested I become a piano teacher. I'd done the odd bit of casual teaching previously, but that had never gotten anywhere, as I was too anxious and only had a keyboard to teach from.

The piano was moved over to my house. The piano I'd had since I was three in my parents' house. It was now officially mine, and I was full of gratitude to be reunited with it. It was a no brainer. I wanted to inspire people like I had been inspired for music all those years ago. There was one problem. I had an anxiety disorder. Being scared of everything is a bit of a problem when you want to be a teacher. I originally decided to state that I specialised in older people simply because I was less terrified of the prospect of teaching them! My other thought was older people tend to have daytime lessons, and I wasn't ready to give up my evenings just yet.

The issue was in 2016, and I was still very anxious. I was still terrified of the phone and even talking to strangers, which was a bit of a problem when it came to getting new clients. Growth was ridiculously slow, and Dr G reassured me that I was just growing gradually, and it would come in time. I had one student for the first few months. Hannah was a friend and university student who fancied learning. She already played a brass instrument so she could read music. She just needed to learn bass clef. I charged mates rates in return for feedback which never actually happened but was also too scared to put myself out there. I registered on a few directories, but enquiries were slow.

I got my first proper student in the summer. Unfortunately, I think I scared her off by Christmas. She had a couple of weeks off and never came back. I bumped into her locally and asked her how she was. She mumbled that she wasn't able to pick up the stuff and didn't want to keep trying. I felt like I'd failed her. Did I get in too heavy too quickly? Did I choose the wrong method to start with?

I also thought I'd be clever and get an app that allowed me to have a business number on my main phone, but the app was glitchy and often cut off potential clients, which didn't help my business. People came and went. Both older people and children would try for a few weeks then drop off again. I was obviously doing something wrong; I was a failure. I wasn't meant to be a piano teacher. However, I was pushed into music so much growing up that I didn't think I was good at anything else either. I was also pregnant around then, so I figured I'd just weather it out and see what was on the other side. I waited, and eventually, two to three years later, people started to find me, and I filled up through word of mouth.

For the academic year 2016/17, I was still part of the student-run music society. I had been an alto in the choir since I was a student, and because I didn't like change, I stuck around indefinitely. I ended up being the only non-student in the choir by the end. 2016 was the year I found the guts to audition as a co-accompanist. It was super exciting but also really nerve-wracking! I found the courage because the conductor at the time was a friend of mine. The chairperson of the society that year was also Hannah, so I felt safe. The first term I did it, the other accompanist was fantastic. I was so inspired by him, but he was as quiet as I was, so I struggled to hold a conversation with him and would admire his talent from more of a distance. The way it worked was one of us played, and the other was a page-turner.

The second term, I carried on as accompanist and Jake took over the director spot. He was the funniest and most talented musician I'd ever met. Everyone thought he was a legend, and he was so quirky and didn't care what people thought. He'd make up comedy songs, and my favourite memory was doing the team photo where he was holding a society pencil, and I was holding my baby Casio keyboard for a joke. It was one of the best years of my life, and I started to feel part of things, even though for every social function, I still got awful social anxiety. Things didn't end up going to plan, though. I fell pregnant in 2016, which meant I didn't get to see to the end of the year as an accompanist.

That final spring concert was amusing. I was waddling across the stage between singing and playing the piano. Some people didn't realise I was pregnant until that point, but I kept going. I even page turned for the massive 'Les Misérables Medley', which the other accompanist messed up halfway through. Those who watched the stream probably didn't see me trying to discreetly conduct him back into time. The look of horror on the conductor's face as he looked over at us was never forgotten.

I had my baby in May 2017, which meant I didn't quite get to the end of the academic year to see those students off. I realised at this point, of course, that I had no chance of growing my business until I'd adjusted to being a mother. At the summer gala concert, I made it over to the hall. I had just about physically recovered from the birth, so I went to watch in the audience but also got social anxiety. Even though I was happy to see everyone, I was too anxious to say hello or strike up a conversation.

I had a couple of opportunities in 2018. Firstly. I'd made a contact while playing at the local National Trust property, and he'd put a poster up in his village, which had found me one of my first official students. He'd given my number to another lady who ran the local memory club for people with dementia. I was really nervous, but I accepted it and drove there once a week to entertain them with my digital keyboard crammed into my tiny yellow car. People gave me great feedback, and although I was socially anxious, they made me feel welcome. I brought my baby to their

Christmas event with my mother-in-law, and we had a lovely time. Sadly, it wasn't too far into the next term that I got a random email saying they could no longer afford me. We parted ways.

Later that summer, an opportunity came up to accompany a choir. Their director was Jake, who was graduating, so he wanted to hand over the reins. Of course, I already knew Jake from the previous year in music society. One of my adult students had told me about the upcoming vacancy and persuaded me to go for it. I got there for the first rehearsal and joined the choir. I really enjoyed it and went back a couple of times. One week they just put me on the spot because Jake couldn't make it that week. I had to do a demonstration there and then. My heart leapt into my mouth and my anxiety triggered majorly. I remember shaking like a leaf but surviving and being jittery and nervous when I spoke. A woman in the choir kept asking awkward questions and I could feel the tears brimming. I just wanted her to stop. She eventually stopped. I took a deep breath. I didn't have a meltdown, but I think she noticed my wobble. They informed me they were going to discuss things, so I was asked to leave the room. I wanted to be their accompanist, but I didn't have the confidence to be their director and I think they spotted that straight away. Over the next couple of weeks, I had a few emails back and forth. It emerged that one of the senior members had asked his professional musician friend to take over, she agreed.

The leader still wanted me to help, so the musician who'd taken the role decided to make me the rehearsal pianist. I had all these grand plans for repertoire, and I was told I would have no say in anything. I was devastated.

That's not what I signed up for. It triggered me, and the email that the new director sent was both condescending and very abrupt. I didn't want to work with anyone who spoke to people like that, so I emailed the choir leader and apologised that I was letting her down, but I wouldn't be able to take the role—that was August 2018.

September 2018 came around, and another opportunity came up. I told myself everything happens for a reason. There was an accompanist job for a choir too. It was only ten minutes down the road, as opposed to a half-hour drive up a mountain and paid ten pounds more per session. I shakily auditioned, but I think I was the only candidate. I answered all the questions, was able to make the people laugh too and I was accepted! I had a trial until Christmas. I, of course, got social anxiety at the Christmas meal, but I was elated to be told I'd passed my trial and was now a permanent accompanist for the local choir.

I never actually got to play any concerts for the choir, but I loved the weekly rehearsals.

ON THE TEACHING FRONT

Despite my inability to communicate properly and grow my business as a piano tutor, I did pick up a girl and her grandmother through a poster that a friendly local guy had put in his village for me. Five years later, the girl is just starting her grade three.

I had ten clients on my books by the end of the first tax year. Dr G suggested I have a goal in mind at the start of my self-employed journey. That was the goal I'd kept in my head. It was a slow and gradual growth, but I had very low expectations. I was so terrified of being judged and always felt inferior to most of my peers who taught piano in the local area.

Out of the ten students, there was the girl that signed up for a block of five, then disappeared after two lessons. One of the younger students was a teenager who was linked to the local cathedral. She was entitled to complementary lessons as part of her involvement in the cathedral choir. She lasted quite a few months, but she struggled to remember things from one lesson to the next, and when she stopped singing in the choir, her free lessons just ended, so she disappeared too.

Since I was still linked to the university, I also picked up a couple of students that way. One tried to take a lesson while wearing really long acrylic nails. I didn't know what to say or do, so I never saw her again after that session. The other university student was a grade eight Trinity Board person. We would struggle to find a mutually free time, then when we did, she would make the same mistakes every week. By the time the semester ended, I think we just got fed up with each other.

I only had the legal two weeks off when I had my baby in May 2017. I didn't try to grow my business, but if anyone enquired, I'd try my best to fit them in. I had twelve students on my books that year, but half of the time, I was severely sleep-deprived and trying to survive by eating something like a coffee bean or a jelly baby before every lesson. I barely knew what I was doing, but a few stuck by me and kept me going, even though I was struggling personally.

The peak of my piano business until lockdown was 2018/19 when I even had a composition student. It was an exciting year as a teacher, but I struggled to retain the younger ones as they dropped off through boredom. Every time someone left, I took it personally and it was getting me down.

That third year of operating, I had twenty people on my books. I was starting to feel a bit more successful but was still unable to get out there and be visible. I'd relied on word-of-mouth and people finding me via vague adverts on local music teacher websites. It was nice when I began to hear local people recommending me. My child started at the school nursery, so I plucked up the courage to ask the headteacher about the possibility of getting involved with the school. He informed me that the big music centre had a monopoly on the local area, so I might want to get in touch via them and see if I could get in that way.

I again plucked up the courage to contact the head of the centre. I didn't get any response back, so I lost faith straight away. I thought they didn't want to know, and I wasn't good enough. Most of their staff were known in the field, had travelled the world, and experienced all kinds of exciting things. Then there was me, the shy piano teacher who didn't have any public experience. The best thing I had in my portfolio was playing background music at a local National Trust property for free and a random wedding I did in 2018—no chance.

However, someone told me the music centre wasn't great at replying, so I should pop in there and try in person. One day I did that. I had a free morning and drove the twenty minutes to get there. The head of the music centre was quite friendly, but I was a nervous wreck. I was so shaky talking to her, she could probably tell. It turned out my email had gone to their spam folder. She apologised and asked me to send over my CV. When I got home, I sent it straight over but heard nothing back. That's it, I thought. I'm obviously not good enough. I may as well resign to the fact that I'll never be recognised as an actual pianist.

In the third year of Michael's degree, he asked if I would be his accompanist. I jumped at the chance. I put my all into that job, and I loved the repertoire. It was so challenging that my fingertips actually started cracking that winter. I even considered finger protectors at one point but quickly realised they weren't practical. I soldiered on and was still very much a perfectionist as far as being a pianist went, except this was my job. I had to play something, so even when I messed up, I had to carry on. A few valuable lessons were learned that year regarding being a pianist, namely that being a perfectionist was not healthy. Michael successfully graduated that summer, so I was completely on my own as a self-employed person for the first time in my life.

Less than a month after Michael finished his course, a close family member was diagnosed with cancer, so I just had to sit on what I had. There was no time to try and expand the business as we had to put all our efforts into keeping the family going. Childcare was fairly minimal, so we just made do with what we had. It didn't do my mental health any good, but there were others more in need than me and I accepted that. September was roughly when the family member got the all-clear—phew! I started to get a few new students like I did every new academic year, and this time it was starting to look up. I had just about enough students to keep me going. I even got asked to teach a girl GCSE composition which was a nice surprise, and we had a couple of great terms doing those projects.

Then lockdown happened. Choir just stopped. No online sessions, nothing.

I lost two-thirds of my students just like that! Some just didn't want to attend online lessons. Others simply said, "See you when it's over." A small proportion tried online, but their internet or technology just wasn't good enough. This left a small handful who were willing, or able, to give online a chance. I didn't have a proper setup at the start of lockdown, so the stand I found at the right height for my iPad was a giant Jenga tower! Yes, my gaming side came through for me, and that Jenga tower came in very handy for what turned into six months of lockdown.

All the guides said you should have multiple cameras at this angle, and your student should have an actual piano and multiple cameras. I believed them at first, and it tipped my anxiety over the edge. I was so nervous in my first week of online teaching. I tried the dual camera approach once, but it confused my student, and my internet didn't like it much either. Straight away, I decided it wasn't worth the hassle. Jenga tower, comfortable iPad, the overall position of me and my piano—done. All my students were happy with that, and I was happy that they showed up, no matter the quality of their set-up. My perfect pitch helped enormously too.

The lessons were at random times in the daytime because there wasn't any school or childcare. Some students had half-size keyboards, some had crackly connections, one even had a broken keyboard at one point, but we made it work because we had to. They needed to keep going just as much as I did. I even got a few more lessons than usual over the summer holidays, when usually I'd have none. However, I'd lost several thousand pounds over the first lockdown. In the August, I had a breakdown about the lack of money.

My proper growth started in the September. I pulled myself together, acquired a proper stand for my iPad, and made a plan. I did more self-development on the business front and threw my all into what I was doing. A curveball was that Michael had come back to do a postgraduate course, and he'd asked specifically for me. I was elated he was back but also felt the need to put my piano plans on hold again. I still wasn't out there. I just relied on word-of-mouth again, and if nothing came, I tried not to care. I appreciated the people that had stuck by me.

In January 2021, we were back in lockdown. There had been two students who couldn't attend online lessons who made it back to me, and I didn't want to lose them again. They were vulnerable, making progress, and I was so proud of what they'd achieved despite the lockdown. This time I taught the vulnerable ones in person, and the others went back to online lessons. It was a hybrid arrangement that worked quite well with my routine, but it was such a relief in mid-April to be able to go back to face-to-face lessons.

During the early 2021 lockdown, I'd reconnected with an old university friend, Sophie. We were both too anxious back then, but we'd occasionally work together on projects. Over the years, we seemed to connect and disconnect. It was strange, and I thought she was weird as she was always missing lectures and disappearing or reappearing months, or sometimes years, down the line. It was anxiety that got in the way. We reconnected properly this time, and I helped her with the tools I'd used to improve my mental health, and I found out she ran a music school that offered piano lessons. She complained about having waiting lists and working too many hours, so I took the leap and offered to take some students off her hands. I gained a couple of permanently online piano students.

After the confidence I'd found in my Facebook community, I was a pianist in my own right. I'd learnt since Christmas that people loved hearing my piano music after spending many years being a perfectionist and afraid that people would judge me and say I wasn't good enough. I played my first full concert live that Christmas as an exclusive for members of my community. The feedback was out of this world! I learnt through playing live online over 2021 that I didn't need to be perfect. I just needed to be confident.

I've got the Visibility Queen to thank for most of my projects and journeys. I was asked to make a guest appearance at a charity event at the end of March, was interviewed on her YouTube channel in April, then launched my first professional website in the May. However, at the end of May, I suffered a small setback. Someone had enquired about an accompanist for their children's exams—grade six and seven. I quoted what I thought was fair, knowing it was under what the Musician's Union recommended. After all, I was inexperienced, so I was willing to go slightly cheaper to get the experience. Except when following up, the mother said that the local music service had offered the same thing cheaper, so they'd be going with them instead. I instinctively apologised and said I understood that she'd chosen someone else. The next day I got a friend request on Facebook. It turned out it was the husband trying to 'call me out' for my pricing. I never accepted him, but I replied to his messages thinking he was enquiring about general piano lessons. He quoted my piano lesson price at me from the website they'd found me on. Accompanist jobs are not the same as teaching a piano lesson. A lot more work is required. I quoted the website link to him, and he never responded after that. I learnt a valuable lesson again that day—know your worth. It majorly triggered my anxiety, but the positive aspect is that it only took me a day to sort my head out. Thanks to my supportive friends and network, I was able to show resilience. Move on. I told myself that better things were yet to come.

I'm not afraid to get out there anymore. This should have been me in February 2016 when I started, but I had so many obstacles and mental health issues to overcome it took me until May 2021 to really start to get there. Onwards and upwards! I now have my own brand and am unique in my field. The Visibility Queen called me the most niche person she'd ever worked with.

My biggest achievement for 2021 was becoming a bestselling author as part of a collaboration with fourteen other women for the book *Seen*. I told the brief story of being the piano tutor who was scared of people and how I eventually found myself, my purpose and my power. I appeared in a local newspaper at the end of November, promoting my big Christmas concert. I ended 2021 with an extensive Christmas campaign, starting with a Victoria Wood inspired Tropic Pianist Gamer's Version of the twelve days of Christmas. I then ended it by playing my first live public concert to forty-one ticket holders in a private Facebook group. The feedback was off the scale! Sadly, the choir I was accompanist for never recovered after lockdown. The memories won't be forgotten, despite the fact that I never got to do a concert with them.

MY FITNESS JOURNEY

Why can't I swim? Anxiety tells me I can't swim, then the logical side of my brain says I can sort of swim, but it's not worth the risk because if it turns out I can't, then I'll drown. The last time I went swimming was probably in 2014. It was the year I got my hair dip-dyed a bright red colour, then the next week I didn't realise that it had reacted with the chlorine, so it faded almost straight away.

Let's rewind a bit first. I learnt to swim when I was around seven years old, and I remember getting a certificate for swimming four widths and being proud. I never liked jumping in because the first time I did, I landed on my toe weirdly and injured it. The instructor told me to stop being a wimp and on the last day of lessons, he put a fake spider in the bottom of the pool. Most of the kids found it funny, but I was terrified of spiders, so it gave me nightmares! At the time, the instructor laughed it off and said I was silly because I should have known that a real spider would have floated.

I took a break from swimming and started other sports instead. In secondary school, physical education lessons undoubtedly involved swimming. They were awkward and embarrassing, and I was put in the baby pool with one other kid who also couldn't swim. That other kid mocked me because I still had armbands. Meanwhile, the rest of the kids were learning to dive in at the deep end, and if it wasn't for the kid with the comments, I would have been quite happy paddling in the baby pool. It became such an awkward class that I started forging letters from my mum to get out of it. Thankfully, it was only year seven. We didn't have to take swimming classes after that.

When I was about fifteen, my mum booked me some more swimming lessons at the local pool where a lad in his twenties was the lifeguard on duty and a lady of similar age was the teacher. It was going well for a few sessions, although I was anxious. I overheard the lad talking to a colleague about the 'ugly girl with the hairy legs', and I knew he was talking about me. I was crushed. My legs had only just become hairy, and I had a skin condition which meant that the hair follicles were more obvious too. It wasn't a good look, but I didn't know any different, and swimming costumes didn't leave much room for imagination. I wasn't slim, but I wasn't that overweight. I was terribly self-conscious, and overhearing mutterings that could have only been aimed at me put me off ever going back.

As an adult, I didn't really swim at all. There was supposed to be a spa day with a friend in 2009, but I forgot my swimming costume. The first family holiday I went on with the in-laws in 2010, the villa had a swimming pool, so I was quite happy until I realised that the country's climate caused me to have nose bleeds, which triggered if I went in the pool!

The next time I went swimming was probably my hen party. I remembered how to doggy paddle, but that was it, so I felt a bit daft, although I tried to enjoy myself because it was my hen party. What I hadn't bargained for was the fact I was so short-sighted I couldn't see much when I took my glasses off. Of course, no one takes their glasses swimming, so off they came, and I put them on a table, and all was good that afternoon. However, the next morning we went for an early morning swim, and I put my glasses on the table again. On coming out of the pool, I grabbed my glasses and went to the sauna. While in the sauna, I noticed my toe was bleeding. I must have sliced it somewhere along the poolside when I wasn't wearing my glasses. I only realised the damage when I went back to my room and got in the shower. It was a pretty deep cut. I managed to stop the bleeding, wrap it up, and pretend nothing had happened. I went to breakfast with the group and said nothing. While I was munching on a black pudding, I overheard a couple of members of staff muttering to each other about a trail of blood from the pool to the sauna and they had no idea who it was. I was so embarrassed that I hid in my corner and made myself as small as possible. We left fairly swiftly after breakfast and still said nothing. They never found out who it was. After that day, one of my friends asked me if I knew that prescription goggles existed. Well, that was me sorted! I ordered some almost straight away.

Public swimming pools majorly triggered me, though. Not just the volume of people, but the chlorine irritated my asthma and skin. I, therefore, wouldn't go near public swimming pools, but I could be persuaded to take a dip if it was in a private spa. For my wedding weekend, we spent quite a bit of time in the spa. I loved the hot tub, the steam room and the sauna It was great fun and also a rare opportunity to have the time to relax with friends. After the wedding, we'd book occasional spa days. I joined my friend Clare for her hen do the following year too. This involved a spa day, but I was anxious for most of that. I tried to enjoy it as best I could. It was about 2015 I realised that people with high blood pressure were advised not to use the steam rooms or the sauna, which put me off ever booking a spa day again. I didn't see the point as that was half the experience. I, therefore, haven't been swimming since then.

I was self-conscious in a swimming costume. I just about found a black tankini that I felt ok wearing, but then I became pregnant and never thought about it again.

Having lost a lot of weight in the last couple of years, none of my clothes fit. So, when an offer of a trek came up with some of my Tropic team, I was excited to connect with them. There was no way I would go swimming in the waterfall as proposed, so when we were there, most took a dip, but I just sat on the side watching. I was perfectly happy but also realised I was probably missing out on the experience a little because of previous anxieties that I hadn't yet overcome.

As a primary school pupil, I was chunkier. I wasn't fat, but I had broad shoulders. I was a rugby player, so it was expected. I was sporty until I was twelve. One of the insults the bullies threw at me at the age of thirteen was that I was fat. Comments at home didn't help—little jibes about how

I could lose a bit of weight. My mum commented it was just puppy fat and I'd grow out of it, except I didn't. I remember as a teenager wanting to keep up with fashion but not being able to afford it. I was always worrying that I was too fat, so I ended up in jeans all the time. I started to wear mostly black because people told me it was slimming. I was so busy attending music-related things, and running between subjects at school, that the actual function of proper exercise was forgotten.

I never had any problems holding down a boyfriend despite being bullied for being fat. Looking at my school photo from year nine and then year eleven, I wasn't fat at all. I look back at my year eleven photo, and I looked slim. Yet, at that time, I was bullied most days about how I looked. I never had the resilience to stand up to those bullies. I just swallowed it and tried not to show them it had got to me while bottling it all up inside. I didn't talk to my parents about it. I would occasionally talk to my brother, but he had his own problems to deal with. As far as I was concerned, he was the favourite anyway. He wasn't fat like me. He knew more than me when it came to general knowledge. My dad always made me think that I was the less clever one.

I felt inferior to everyone at home and school, and I didn't exercise. My parents used to go for walks regularly, but I hated joining them as I found it boring. I did enjoy playing badminton at school. Physical education lessons and memories of year seven and eight hockey were fun but also horrible. Bullies targeted me, but I tried to fight back. I hated netball because it was a girl sport. I was rubbish at rounders because I wanted to play cricket.

As part of my Duke of Edinburgh Bronze Award, I did take up tennis, but that was fairly short-lived, as the girls from the private school picked on me, "Oh, a fourteen-year-old who can't play tennis. HA HA!" I tried to learn, but I eventually became too anxious to attend, so I dropped off the radar after my award criteria was met. I was too scared to report it to the coach, so when I saw him in town, my mum would cheerily wave to him while I ducked into the shadows and hoped he hadn't spotted me!

By the time I made it to university, exercise wasn't even in the equation of life. I generally liked walking everywhere and couldn't yet drive, so I kept sort of fit that way. Halfway through my degree, I started online gaming, which was essentially the end of me going to most places. I spent fourteen hours a day on that game for a good six months, and in that process, I didn't realise the long-term health implications it could have on me.

From that period of life, I ended up with dry eyes, repetitive strain injury, a stiff back and shortened hamstrings. At the time, I didn't think about it, and I just carried on regardless. During the summer of first and second year, I did have a long commute to my summer job, which got me walking again and tired me out, but then it was back to the dirge of outcast uni life.

At the end of my third year, I picked up a PlayStation 2. I'd heard there was a dance mat game where you could put your own songs in, so I was sold. I used to dance off calories and justify eating junk food. I felt so much better about myself, and it was halfway through that time that I met Dr G. It's true that when you start to love yourself, other people will find you. He found me when I stopped looking. I'd just found my way out of my depression and was starting to be comfortable with being single when the two boys crossed my path. However, Liam got there before Dr G did.

Once Dr G and I started dating, our first joint present that Christmas was a *Wii.* It wasn't long before we got the *Wii Fit,* which was my new obsession. I loved it, but like with all video games, I tended to play them for a fixed amount of time, then the novelty wore off. I was like this with *Wii Fit, EA Active* and *EA Active 2.* I'd properly give them a go but eventually drop off again.

I also joined a gym in 2009 because the housemate, Ed, who was living with us, was a gym nut and I thought if he could do it, so could I. However, I got super anxious that year, and after a month, I stopped going to the gym. I then attended yoga classes around 2012. I used to go to the Anglican Chaplaincy and do a lunchtime class. I enjoyed it until I injured myself doing an over-enthusiastic downwards facing dog.

Eventually, we hit 2013. "I'm anxious because I'm fat," was the actual line I used to plead with my doctor just after my diagnosis of Generalised Anxiety Disorder. On advice from the mother-in-law, I asked my doctor if I could have a referral to the gym based on my diagnosis. I was assigned a personal trainer who specialised in rehabilitation and referrals. I was given slots in the local village gym. I was anxious, but I was also taken care of, so I started to get into the gym a bit more again. The personal trainer taught me how to use the equipment, and I joined her circuits class on certain days too. I was the only person under sixty, but I enjoyed it anyway.

From that, I started to enjoy the more active activities again and started playing badminton, having enjoyed that at school. My sister-in-law joined me, and we made a couple of friends along the way. I was awful at staying in touch with people. We joined the badminton club at the local gym, but as soon as I stopped going to the weekly sessions, I lost touch with them, as I was simply too afraid to send messages to stay in touch.

When I got the housing office maternity cover, I used the opportunity to join the university gym. I was really into it for a few months, but it was always a rush as I did it between work and evening Welsh classes, which ended up with me buying takeaways straight after the gym, which defeated the point! By the time I got the private office job, I'd given up with the gym. I did try to join a rounders team in the summer, but it never got off the ground as it kept raining.

Later in 2015, I started seeing a sports rehabilitation person about my chronic back pain. This only came about because I went for a massage in a local beauty salon, and the lady treating me advised me that what I needed was more than what she was able to help me with. She recommended the sports rehabilitation lady, as she was able to overcome sciatica thanks to this person. The sports lady treated me right up until lockdown. When I first started seeing the sports lady, she recommended I start Pilates run by her friend. I booked some one-to-one sessions with the Pilates lady very soon afterwards. I was anxious driving up to her house at the top of Anglesey, but just as I was getting more used to it, she recommended I join her group classes instead. Once I'd walked out of my office job, I was on very low income again, so she was trying to help me save money. I was anxious starting classes, but the people next to me on the mats were friendly and would chat to me. My anxiety stayed with me until lockdown. It wasn't obvious to everyone, but I always used to pick a particular corner of the room to be in for the session. It was usually near the door, so I could potentially escape if I needed to. Pilates moved from a little hut in Beaumaris to a full studio in Llangefni at the end of 2016. It was less claustrophobic, but I still picked a specific corner near the door.

2016 was the year of *Pokémon GO*! That got me up and out of the house for walks. My friend Ross was a lodger that summer, so he and I used to go chasing Pokémon while Dr G was at work. I felt pretty fit after that summer, and then I had three years of sighted guide work from the September. Ten thousand steps a day was part of the job for most of Michael's first year, but in September 2016, I also found out that I was pregnant.

The pregnancy went as well as it could. No sickness and I was doing my ten thousand steps a day and was careful what I ate. I was probably the healthiest I'd ever been, except the pregnancy changes the body in ways you don't expect.

2017-2019 was, therefore, a period of change. Anxious me didn't like change. Mentally I tried to fight it and struggled to adjust to being a mum. I was still working with Michael, but it's safe to say for his second year, I wasn't mentally there. I was in survival mode. The last thing on my mind was being healthy and exercising. Until September 2019, I survived on sugar due to caffeine already being banned. I went for occasional walks but often had days of no exercise whatsoever. I still did weekly Pilates classes, so it could have been worse.

I crashed and burned in August 2019. I was getting regular heartburn at night but just moaning about it and not sleeping. I ignored the signs, but it was only another two weeks before I ended up in hospital and another few weeks before I regained control over my life. It was October 2019. *Ring Fit Adventure* came out for Nintendo Switch, and it was the life-changing game I never knew I needed!

I'd already pre-ordered it without thinking, as I'd loved *Wii Fit* and *EA Active* back in the day, so this was an automatic buy for me. I started by doing five days a week. I would do an hour of exercise every session, which was thirty active minutes in a game. At the time, my child was still having afternoon naps, so this was perfect.

This was the start of me being a consistency queen! I kept it up until lockdown. At peak, I lost just over two stone and was the slimmest and fittest I'd been as an adult. I even lost my bingo wings—I was ecstatic! This was key to getting body confident for the first time in my life! At that point, I still didn't like being in photographs unless they were group arrangements. I was still wearing all black, and I was still anxious about everything else.

I completed adventure mode on *Ring Fit Adventure* in January 2020 and created four custom lists that had a good overall workout. However, I avoided squats as they never seemed to register properly on the game. I tried to start Parkrun UK when my brother came to visit. We managed two at Penrhyn Castle before everything shut down. When lockdown hit, I obviously had nowhere to go, so I upped my workouts on *Ring Fit Adventure* to seven days a week. I'd usually do three custom lists, which would take me to just over thirty active minutes. I'd do the fourth custom list on the odd occasion I had time. My child had stopped having afternoon naps by then, so he was either at childcare or would sit and watch me.

In Summer 2020, I bought myself a hula hoop. I watched a couple of YouTube videos and learnt how to do basic hoop with a normal (non-weighted) hoop. I've only ever been able to do it clockwise so far, though.

As things started to open up after the first lockdown, I had a term where the Pilates classes came back. (I struggled to engage with the virtual zoom sessions during lockdown.) The ladies all told me I looked fantastic, and over the summer, I'd found my LLL leggings too, so I turned up in funky leggings from that day forward. The Pilates classes stopped again over Christmas, but I was also starting to find *Ring Fit Adventure* too easy, so I wanted to change it up a bit.

On Boxing Day 2020, I downloaded *Fitness Boxing 2*. I fancied a change, and this was the cardio I was essentially missing from *Ring Fit Adventure*. I kept it going seven days a week. I alternated between the two. I'd miss an odd day here or there as I became a key worker. Michael had returned for his postgraduate degree, so we were able to have some in-person sessions between January and April.

I began to change things again around Easter. I started going for more walks outdoors, going to the beach and other walks. I also downloaded *Zumba: Burn it Up* and got back into doing *Yoga Master,* which I'd downloaded the previous autumn but not looked at properly. In June, I also participated in a hula hooping challenge for fifteen minutes every day. I realised that my odd bit of hooping over the last year showed I'd been the weird one who counted rotations of hoop rather than time the spinning. Once I got the hang of the challenge, I realised I'd only really been lasting five minutes here and there, so fifteen minutes was a massive increase. About four weeks in, I did fifteen minutes without dropping the hoop for the first time. I usually do it to a feel-good music playlist on Spotify. It's great for raising the vibes!

These days, I alternate between *Ring Fit Adventure, Fitness Boxing 2, Knockout Home Fitness, Yoga Master* and *Zumba: Burn It Up* (all on Nintendo Switch), plus attending weekly Pilates classes, fifteen minutes of hula hooping most days, and walking to take in the beautiful landscapes in my local area. During term time the walk can be as simple as the school run, but every time I go out for a day or afternoon, I get a decent walk in, so on those days, I do my hula hooping in the evening.

I'm not at my target weight just yet, but the main achievement for lockdown was not putting any weight back on again. I was proud that I was able to maintain and even lose a bit here and there. My proudest achievement was I'd got fit by video games without setting foot in a gym.

FASHION & STYLE

Growing up with overprotective parents meant not being able to keep up with my peers. This could have been a good thing given that some of the people at school were drinking by the age of thirteen, wearing makeup when not at school and getting piercings. I just wasn't allowed. Being sent to various after school clubs, music lessons, and ensembles meant that I didn't have time to think about anything else, but it also didn't stop me from wishing I could do what everyone else seemed to be doing. I wasn't allowed makeup, and jewellery was minimal. I'd often have hand-knitted cardigans from my mum's older sister. These could be funky but about as unfashionable as you could imagine. I remember my mum still buying me clothes until I was fifteen.

I think it was my thirteenth birthday, and I'd been allowed to invite a few friends over to watch a film. My mum used to make hot dogs and ice cream sodas and buy a caterpillar cake. It was a birthday on a budget, but it was still special even though my mum had explicitly stated that under no circumstances could I wear nail varnish or any makeup at all. I was miffed but knew I didn't have a choice. However, a friend who turned up to my birthday party brought some glittery nail varnish. My mum left us alone to watch the film, so my friend painted my nails. By the time my mum realised, it was already done. She was annoyed, but she also admitted defeat. She had to buy me some nail varnish remover, and because she didn't believe in waste, she let me have nail varnish after that. I used to wear clear nail varnish most of the time at school. We weren't allowed nail varnish, but I learnt that no one could tell if it was good quality. My cousin bought me my first nail varnish—it was a dark purple glitter. I still have that bottle somewhere for sentimental value. The first varnish I bought myself was a fluorescent orange colour. My mum hated it, but I painted my toes with it so that school couldn't tell I'd painted my nails.

By the time I left for university, I had a drawer full of nail varnishes, mainly silvers, purples, blues and blacks, fluorescent orange, a couple of reds, and plenty of glitter. I would paint my nails most of the time but always got annoyed that it would chip easily, so I would revert to clear or basic silver glitter most of the time. I grew up as a tomboy, but one thing I always loved doing on the girly side was getting my nails done.

I had my nails filed and polished for my wedding, but I didn't know about gel nails until 2013. I thought to have gel, you had to have acrylics, and I hated the thought of having fake nails. It was roughly 2014/15 when I had a complete break from the piano as I worked full-time in an office. Having discovered a lovely lady who did shellac on natural nails, I enjoyed seeing her a bit more regularly during those years whilst being able to keep my nails naturally long. My favourite design was usually a diagonal bright blue or purple with silver glitter. Sometimes I would be too scared to message her because I thought I'd left it too late, so I'd go to another local salon over Christmas and get gel nails done there. The diagonal technique was obviously an artistic thing from the original lady, but I didn't realise and asked this nail technician to do it. I shared a picture for her to work from and I could see her getting stressed because she couldn't work out how it was done. I felt bad for her, but I was too scared to say anything. That was the most awkward nail appointment I ever had.

After that, I went back to the original lady, except the full-time job ended in September 2015. Consequently, my income dropped too. I had to stop getting my nails done regularly, but I was still her regular. I'd pop up, maybe once a year, but she'd always remember me. I was chuffed that she remembered me as I was so convinced I was a nobody back then. I would get my nails done twice at Christmas, but in more recent years, I'd started getting them done in a local chain store because she was providing her services from her house, and it was a bit more of a trek.

Then lockdown happened. I didn't bother even painting my nails for most of it, but about halfway through the first lockdown, I won a prize at a local online networking event. It was for another network marketing company. The only thing they sold that my own company didn't sell was hairbrushes and nail varnish, so that's exactly what I chose.

Fast forward to summer 2021, and I was reunited with the original nail technician. We had a great catchup and finally linked up after my being too afraid to ask to add her on social media previously. She'll always wave me off with a smile and a 'See you next year".

One thing I was definitely not allowed to do was get my ears pierced. I'd ask my parents every so often, but it would always be a resounding no, or when I was eighteen. It got tiresome, but I eventually gave up asking. In my mid-teens, I tried magnetic or clip-on earrings. They were always really uncomfortable, and the styles weren't anything I liked, but I just wanted to fit in with my peers, most of whom had their ears pierced as children.

I was nearly eighteen, but with my birthday in June and the sixth form leavers' party before then, I finally persuaded my parents to let me have my ears pierced. They let me do it slightly too late, though. I'd visualised and even bought the perfect earrings I wanted to wear to the leavers' party, but I had to leave the piercing studs in for so many weeks, and those weeks weren't over by the time the party came round. I was gutted.

At least by the time I went to university, I could wear whatever earrings I liked. I liked twirly ones or coloured studs. As I entered my third year at university, I'd mentioned in the summer that I wanted to get my top ear pierced. My mum said she'd disown me if I did. At that point, I knew I was an adult at age twenty and could technically do whatever I liked. The first week back at university, I went and got my top ear done. It was the left side because I tended to sleep on my right side. I originally wore a basic stud in the top, and then it changed to a ring with a tiny bead for quite a few years. Through lockdown, I changed it to a rainbow heart to signify positivity and love.

My general earrings got even funkier too. Through networking during lockdown, I met so many fellow small business owners, one of which makes custom earrings. Every Sunday, Sharkie & Bear does a Sunday Funday where I tune into the group, keep an eye out for any special pairs that I particularly love, and then jump in when they come up. I have approximately twenty pairs so far and love wearing them for their colours and uniqueness!

Jewellery was generally discouraged, as my mum didn't like it. She only wore the delicate gold watch she'd had as a wedding gift from my dad, plus her plain gold wedding band. They never got engaged; they just got married, so simple it was.

I always liked my bangles, though. In year five, we used to have school fairs where other children would sell friendship bracelets. These particular ones were made out of old tights (or that type of fabric) and came in all sorts of bright colours. I used to wear them in year six because all my friends wore them.

I usually had some kind of bracelet on, but at secondary school, we weren't allowed to wear anything like that until sixth form. By the time sixth form came around, I was collecting jelly bracelets in all sorts of colours and even a barbed-wire styled one to mark that I was a Mosher. I also liked power bead bracelets for different symbols of well-being. In that sense, it was the early noughties, and I was able to keep up with accessories in the fashion world. I was also very fond of my mood ring, and it seemed to always stay on dark blue, which became my favourite colour. As a student at university, I had a favourite ring. I'd usually wear a roman numerals ring on my right hand all the time. I wore that for many years until I started putting on weight, and it no longer fitted.

I loved wearing necklaces, and from my mid-teens, my mum let me collect the leather ones with charms on them, so I had all sorts, ranging from Chinese symbols to dragons and amethysts. I loved my necklaces! When I went to a Christian festival in my late teens, Jonesy and I would often be found in the craft tent making necklaces that I could keep. They were always special to me, as he'd designed them and I'd made them up. However, one year I thought our creation was perfect and wore it all the time at the festival. When we got home, my mum laughed and said she was sorry to tell me, but I was wearing a phallic symbol around my neck! I didn't know what that meant, so I looked it up and was mortified. Lesson learnt—don't make a necklace with a pair of balls and a stiff dangly heart. Jonesy found it hilarious when I told him. By the time we split up, I found it too painful to wear the ones we'd made together, but I kept them safely in a shoebox as they held great memories, and I was always sentimental.

I started wearing proper silver by the time I was with Dr G. An old school friend had gifted me a little heart on a necklace for my eighteenth birthday, so I'd started to wear that as my everyday necklace. In time, my partner and his parents bought me different pieces of silver. He also gave me my Clogau Welsh dragon as my wedding day present.

In 2009, I also started to collect Pandora charms as they were new to the UK market, and I loved the idea that you could tell a story with your bracelet. I completed the first one in a couple of years as I'd buy them when I was out and about on road trips or shopping. I collected Pandora for a few years before noticing other fashions, tapping into Nomination and Notch over lockdown. I love the colours and the storytelling aspect of each one, and that they're all completely different too.

The other accessories I loved when I was much younger were Alice bands, but I found they gave me earache, so I had to stop wearing them. I also associated them with small children after getting bullied in year seven for wearing them. I loved more ornate hair clips when I was a student. My friend had bought me a Victorian-style lace-effect hair clip, so I used to wear that to most of my music concerts. I always had a thick fringe as a small child. My mum thought it made me look cute, but as I hit puberty, I hated it. When I was ten, I had my longish hair cut into a bob. Looking back, I looked ridiculous. At that age, I was playing rugby and football, so I always had broad shoulders. The bob just made me look big. Of course, it took a couple of years to grow it out again, so after that, I've always kept it long.

I was quite sweaty as a teen, so my fringe would stick to my forehead and cause spots. When I was fourteen, I randomly decided one day to cut my hair, and I started with the fringe. I made it so it was just a few thick strands. I also put my long hair into plaited pigtails and cut them straight across at the bottom—what a mess! My mum was horrified. She took me to the hairdressers to get it sorted out, and the hairdresser just laughed. I cringe when I look back at photographs. In my year nine photo, I have a greasy looking hairstyle, with a silly little fringe pinned back by tiny butterfly clips. We didn't get a lot of pocket money; I think it was about seventy pence per week when my boyfriend was getting thirty pounds a week, so I'd steal a tiny butterfly clip once a week from the local pharmacy. I think the chemist got wise as they installed a camera and didn't let anyone in and out unless they were buying something, so I just disappeared. I never got called up about it, but they were only pennies. I didn't like the guilt it caused, so that was the only time I went shoplifting. By the time I was fifteen, I'd got rid of the fringe completely. I kept asking for purple hair too, but I didn't realise that to get true colour, I'd have to bleach my almost black hair, which scared me off the idea.

When I passed my GCSEs, my mum gave me a present—I could get my hair highlighted purple. I was so excited! The result was subtle, with hints of red, but I was just grateful she let me do something interesting with my hair. A week later, when term started, most people at school didn't notice so as usual, I just blended into the background.

When I went to university, I was free, I was an adult, and I could do what I liked. In my first year, I discovered henna hair dye. I tried to dye my hair, making a mess of the en-suite in my student halls. I didn't really do anything with my hair in second year, as I spent most of it in my bedroom playing online games.

In third year I dyed it jet black. There's only one picture of my hair after I'd done it. I thought I looked very pale and deathly. I also knew I had to live with it until it grew out. I had spent the best part of a year only going between my bedroom, lectures and pub lunches, so this wasn't too difficult.

By the time I met my third boyfriend, Liam, he loved my more gothic look. He complimented me if I wore all black and said he loved it when I straightened my hair, so I used to straighten my hair and wear black if we ever went out together. But it wasn't me; it was just me trying to please the boyfriend.

Although I met Dr G at the same time as Liam, Dr G only got to know me online initially. My hair had gone back to its natural colour by the time we started dating. He liked me just as I was. I had naturally wavy hair and lots of it, but I'd usually wear it up as it was very frizzy. I was a low maintenance type of person. I only got it dyed again in 2014 when dip-dye was the in-thing. I got my hair dyed red at the bottom, and it looked amazing. I was the most confident I'd felt in a while. I was a size twelve for the first time as an adult, and I was loving life, even though I had only just been diagnosed with my anxiety disorder.

I was happy with dip-dye because it meant roots weren't a thing, but I made a massive mistake. One week later we went on holiday. The first full day was spent in a spa. I didn't realise that the hair dye reacted with the chlorine in the water, so most of the red washed out that afternoon. I was gutted! I'd paid quite a bit for it and only realised when I put my head on the guest house pillow that it had pink spots on it. Dr G thought it was hilarious, but I was so mortified I never owned up to it and very sheepishly checked out of the guest house the next morning.

That was the last time I did anything with my hair, and it wasn't really on my list after I had my baby in 2017. My hair went thicker, then thinner, and I never knew where I stood with it. When I joined Tropic Skincare as an ambassador, I decided to try the haircare range. Although it wasn't completely for me, I found a combination that worked, so although my hair is thinner than it used to be and is going grey, I'm more confident overall than I ever was before.

I wasn't allowed makeup when everyone else was experimenting with it. Things like fake tan just weren't on my radar. I always had the English rose complexion, which made me unusual being half Chinese. Paleness actually suited me with my rosy cheeks. When I got to sixth form and had my purple highlights, my mum managed to be persuaded to let me try some things. I'd go into town with friends during lunchtimes from school and buy the odd (clear) lip gloss and some eye makeup. I never really got to grips with makeup, though. No one taught me how to apply it properly, and I didn't understand why eye shadow never stayed on my eyes. By the time I got to university, I got frustrated with eye shadow. I wanted to keep up with my peers, so the best solution for me was to buy glitter pots instead of powder and just use that instead, with waterproof mascara, because I could get emotional at any point in time. Even then, I'd only wear it when I went 'out out', which wasn't very often.

This carried on until I was planning my wedding. It was expected that a bride would book a makeup artist and hairdresser for their wedding, so I did exactly that. The makeup artist introduced me to full makeup and advised me on colours and how they worked. The same month I picked up a starter kit from Bare Minerals. The advantage of that was that it came with a DVD tutorial, so I was able to watch it and learn how to apply it all properly. That same box was with me for the decade. I'd occasionally add eye shadows to it if I found colours I liked, but I generally played it safe and always stuck with clear lip gloss.

Joining Tropic changed all that. Sustainable and refillable makeup, naturally derived too, was a no-brainer for me. It turns out that makeup should only last about a year, not ten! I did a direct swap in summer 2020, and I colour matched all my old makeup for the new palette. I experimented in August and showed my collection to my community. A fellow ambassador suggested colour matching from an expert. I also made it my mission to try all the coloured lip glazes in my December campaign. To my surprise, one of my followers piped up and said I really suited the Toffee Spice, which was one of the bolder shades! This is now my go-to when I'm feeling bold. Meanwhile, the colour match person recommended the Cherry on Top lipstick, which is quite a bright pinkish-red. I absolutely loved it! I became fairly comfortable showing off elements of makeup online. In August 2021, I had a colour expert do a matching event in my community, and she recommended me the Hot Poppy shade of lipstick. In September 2021, attended events started popping up again, and with my newfound confidence, I went to a literary lunch that October. I wore a full face of makeup with the Hot Poppy lipstick, my Alice Popsy dress, a wine-coloured petticoat, and glittery black boots. Despite coming down with a cold, I felt stunning that day.

When I was younger, I often had knitted woolly things from my relatives, and I remember I loved dresses. I had a favourite purple Minnie Mouse dress that I liked to wear when I was about nine. I was into football more in years five and six, so by the time I was eleven, I decided I didn't like dresses and lived in leggings because my Nana didn't approve of jeans. As I got further into secondary school, I realised everyone else was wearing them, and my leggings were very outdated. It wasn't until I was nearly fifteen that I was finally allowed to pick my own outfit from the shop. I remember my mum took me clothes shopping in York. I started with an orange and navy-blue fleece with a navy t-shirt with a sports slogan on it. Paired with black trousers, it was about as far away from fashion as I could be, but at least I was able to choose something myself.

The great thing about school is you have to wear a uniform, except for the very rare non-uniform days when I had year seven's fashion disaster of leggings with a baggy, rainbow coloured, woolly jumper. I got ripped to shreds with the verbal jibes, and I started turning up in plainer clothes. I just about managed to get the full denim setup for one non-uniform day but still got picked on, so it made no difference what I wore.

For my sixteenth birthday, my friends organised a trip to the Trafford Centre. They were the type of friends who encouraged me to buy stuff, so I bought some lace-up jeans and a union jack t-shirt in the sale. I think I wore them once, but the t-shirt disappeared fairly quickly after my mum commented that it was a bit short, and I was a bit big for it. The jeans stuck around, though, but since they were a smaller size, I rarely fitted them without having a muffin top, which ate away at my already low self-confidence.

Sixth form was all about the Moshers. I didn't really know what a Mosher was, but my friend who rode the bus was one, and I admired her style. I tried to copy her so I could blend in. I started wearing black with accents of colour matched with black or coloured accessories. I remember being fond of a particular cardigan. It was a weird texture, but it wasn't itchy because the fluff was a stiffer type of wool. I used to wear it under my blazer in the colder weather, as the sixth form uniform was suits.

At university, I just settled into jeans and black t-shirts. I loved wearing the university and society hoodies and polo shirts, but it was always jeans. I didn't even like shorts in the summer. I was super self-conscious about my legs because of being bullied at school, and the effort of hair removal took me half the day and was messy. Towards my third year, I discovered shrugs, so I used to wear jeans with black vest tops and shrugs to look a little bit smarter.

It was at the start of my master's degree that I met Dr G. He introduced me to epilators, which I've used ever since. It still took me half a day to sort, and I only did it when I felt I had to. Dr G always loved me for who I was and wasn't bothered by stuff like that. I was always really self-conscious when going out, so when it was too hot outside, I'd put time aside to epilate my legs so I could wear shorts. I'd always be self-conscious about sweat, as I perspired a lot. That's why I only ever wore black t-shirts so that no one could tell.

This carried on until lockdown. I'd lost weight after my illness in September 2019 and started aiming for a specific target weight. I'm still not there yet, but I know I will when I focus properly. The main priority is to maintain, as I've now got my confidence which means I'll wear dresses and colourful leggings. I've not touched my jeans since August 2020. In June 2020, I discovered a certain brand of dresses called Popsy. They helped my confidence, and I would get compliments online when I shared pictures. I started featuring them on my live videos in my community—adding a bit of lip glaze or lipstick added to the feelings of being genuinely confident. One thing I noticed after losing weight was that I perspired less. I switched to Tropic's deodorant in August 2019 and never looked back.

I didn't want to sweat or go walking in a dress, and given the chance, I love going for walks and taking in the local views. I didn't want to go back to jeans. They were too restrictive and didn't cope well when it rained. I noticed that those buying the dresses also loved a particular brand of leggings called Lucy Locket Loves.

I now save the dresses for my live sessions or if I'm going somewhere nice (that doesn't include walking), and the rest of the time, I live in leggings. I'm known as the mum with the funky leggings at my Pilates class and outside the school gates. It's a great conversation starter too! I always liked my colours; I just didn't know how to wear them.

When face to face events started back properly in September 2021, I would choose a Popsy dress to wear for every event. If I had to drive longer distances, I would wear leggings, then quickly get changed in my car. The September event was incredible. I wore my star Ally Popsy dress and decided to wear my star-themed hat that I'd made a few years ago. I was the most eccentrically dressed person that day, but it was my first test of having confidence in real life, and I smashed it! People loved my outfit, I loved my outfit, and I was truly happy, especially when I won the Queen of Progress Award for everything I'd achieved since I started my journey in the first lockdown.

During that term, I had the Tropic Glambassadors event, the aforementioned literary lunch, and the book launch when I became a best-selling author. Christmas was busy with networking events, all of which I carefully chose a Popsy dress for the occasion. I also experienced new things, like a Visionary Experience Day, so anything where I was more active, I would choose my best leggings to wear for the day. I am never wearing anything too plain ever again.

SCARING MYSELF INTO DRIVING

I actually had to learn to drive twice. All my friends in sixth form learnt to drive when they were seventeen. It wasn't even an option for me, my parents couldn't afford it, and I wasn't allowed to have a Saturday job to save up for it myself. When I hit third year at university, having nearly failed second year, I decided I'd better buck my ideas up if I wanted to get anywhere, so with this came the idea of learning to drive. I got my provisional driving licence and was good to go. There was a reasonably priced guy who popped up on Facebook, so I contacted him and booked some lessons in.

I remember that I was jittery and nerve-wracked for more than half the driving lessons. I'd be doing thirty miles per hour in the fifty zones, and once, I even did fifty miles per hour in the thirty zone. Initially, I couldn't seem to get the concept of changing gear at the same time as steering, but thankfully it was a dual controlled car. It was the twentieth lesson, and we were nowhere near ready for a test. I'd been having them every Monday afternoon just before a lecture, which had also had a negative impact on that entire module due to anxiety. I couldn't concentrate on what was already something majorly out of my comfort zone: standing in front of an audience waving a conductor's baton. I learnt the techniques early on in the term, but as the term advanced, the developments made me more anxious. By the time of the exam, I was a complete wreck!

It was one fateful Monday afternoon, and I decided I'd had enough. I obviously wasn't meant for driving. I learnt to drive in Bangor. Hill starts were aplenty and so were the thirty miles per hour zones. Roundabouts were terrifying, and Coed Mawr hill was the stuff of nightmares. That twentieth lesson, the driving instructor decided to try and teach me three-point turns on a particular road, Trem Elidir. I'll never forget it. I got halfway through the manoeuvre and panicked. I pressed the accelerator instead of the brake. The instructor jammed on the brakes then an awkward silence followed. Eventually, he looked at me with a glare and said, "If this wasn't a dual controlled car, we would have fallen down that slope and died!"

I was mortified and horrified! I could never drive again. He dropped me off after the lesson and I never contacted him again. I think he was glad I didn't go back. I was hopeless! That one line about us nearly dying scarred me for life. Fast forward to 2010, and we were looking at finally moving out of Bangor and on to Anglesey. Dr G told me I needed to learn to drive and should try again, as he knew that I would feel too isolated if I didn't have access to a car, as I was terrified of public transport, whether that be bus, taxi or train.

I searched the internet for a female instructor, as my gut instinct told me a woman would be more likely to understand me. I found a lady who specialised in nervous people. It just had to be her I contacted her and booked my first lesson. The advantage this time was that Dr G had been driving for ten years by then, so he was able to act as my secondary instructor. This was a blessing and a hindrance at the same time.

I had another twenty lessons with the new instructor, but this time it worked out. I had weekly lessons but also had practise in Dr G's car. The issue here was that my instructor's car (a Toyota Yaris) needed to have the clutch in to start the engine and Dr G's car (Ford Fiesta) didn't.

I still freaked out randomly in the lessons, but she was a lot better equipped to calm me down and talk me through it. I scared myself into being able to do hill starts on Coed Mawr, and roundabouts became doable. I'd finally understood the action of changing gear AND steering! My theory test was booked for the March, and I was ready.

I failed the hazard perception section because I was too cautious. I saw things that weren't there, apparently. Meanwhile, my brother was learning to drive at the same time, so we kept competing with each other. He passed his theory test first time, so he was winning. I retook the test a couple of weeks later and passed. Onwards to the practical test. My brother failed his practical test three times. I passed first time, but my test wasn't that simple.

The night before the test, I had a night terror. They were quite rare, but they were always the same. This was also the last time I ever experienced one.

Night Terror: You think you're awake, and a massive spider with its body as big as your face lands on your face, and you can't breathe. The legs are everywhere. You find breath, you scream! But you're also asleep, and your boyfriend lying next to you is frightened. The guest you have that weekend doesn't hear anything—weird! Your boyfriend shakes you awake, but you are pretty traumatised and now have to attend your driving test on just a few hours of sleep!

I sat the test in the instructor's car, as that was the car I was supposed to be used to. However, I'd practised in Dr G's car in the lead up to the exam. The examiner sat in the passenger seat with his clipboard and asked me a few questions. I was ridiculously shaky, but he helped me calm down a bit. He indicated that we were ready to begin the test. I put the key in the ignition and turned it. Nothing happened. I started to panic. I tried it again—nothing. I looked at the examiner and he gave me a blank look. He got out of the car and came round to the driver's side. Just as he opened the door, I remembered. My instructor's car needed the clutch in to start the engine. I'd never been more mortified in my life. I went bright red, apologised profusely and was about to burst into tears, assuming I'd failed my driving test. The examiner chuckled, "Oh, don't worry, we haven't officially started yet. Shall we start now?" I'd never let out the biggest sigh of relief in my life! I hadn't failed. We just had a hiccup, it wasn't over yet, but it was a clean slate to begin my test. Off we went. I was shaky, but I survived. I nearly missed a turning off the dual carriageway, but I did it! Thirteen minor errors but no majors.

I shared Dr G's car for the first six years. My brother

had to do his driving test three times before he passed, so I won. He then got his first car, so the final score was Bro 2 - 1 Me. Fair game. I really enjoyed the 'new world' that driving gave me, although, for the first few years, it could be annoying having to get up to take Dr G to work just so I could use the car.

It took me a couple of longer trips to realise that a car needed petrol to run. I remember driving to Wrexham, and I hadn't realised the warning light had come on for the fuel tank. At a certain point, Dr G asked when the light had come on. I had no idea. I panicked! "Oh my God, we're going to run out of petrol on the dual carriageway!" Dr G laughed nervously. "You'll just have to 'roll' to the nearest petrol station then." We just about made it. I remember sitting in the driver's seat while Dr G filled up the car with petrol. An older man came over to my side and was quite aggressive. He was fed up with waiting and wanted me to move. I was shaking and gestured sorry but didn't wind my window down. Thankfully, he backed off when he saw Dr G coming back. I nervously left the forecourt, and we went on our way.

In Summer 2010, we went on our first family holiday. On the way back, we stopped at my sister-in-law's. I drove home, and the suspension fell off his car as I left her estate. We had no idea what it was. It just made a massive clunk noise. He got out of the car, looked at it, assumed we'd just run over it and left it in the road. The garage later confirmed it was the suspension and we were lucky we were still able to drive it.

Summer 2011, just before my twenty-fifth birthday, Dr G persuaded me to sign up for Pass Plus to give me more driving confidence. (It was free for under twenty-fives.) The first bit was watching a video about the dangers of driving, and the second bit was where an instructor took you on a road trip to practise more advanced driving skills. We drove from Wrexham to Manchester United's football ground before he realised that there was an event on, so we couldn't go into the grounds. He seemed to be a bit colour blind too, as on a roundabout, he told me to follow the blue car. I followed his instructions, but he shouted I'd gone the wrong way, then gestured towards the silver car that was going off at the next exit. He did apologise after we completed the journey, thankfully.

Around 2012, Dr G's car was starting to fall apart. In the spring, we got stuck halfway up a one-way hill and caused a traffic jam. We had to wait to be towed back home. For my hen do, the car was playing up again. I remember it nearly broke down, and the engine warning light kept coming on, so we had to drive a maximum of fifty miles per hour everywhere, which made a fun trip around Chester and home again. I was so terrified I might crash.

My mum and brother came up for a little holiday that summer, and I thought I'd take them for a trip around Anglesey. We got stuck at the first stop, Rhosneigr, where the wheel had started to come off on the rear side. My mum found a local garage, and we asked if he could help. It was his day off, but he saw how distressed I was and said to leave it with him, and he would sort it. He wasn't allowed to let me drive off either, so we were stuck in Rhosneigr for the rest of the afternoon. He did indeed sort it, so thankfully, we made it home in time for tea. The following summer, Dr G finally upgraded his car. We collected it on the way home from a close friend's wedding in 2013.

Fast forward to Christmas 2016, when my parents offered me my mum's old car. I was so grateful I could finally have my own run-around. A new world opened up to me. I had just become self-employed, and having my own car gave me so many more possibilities and flexibility.

Alas, by exam season in 2018, my car was starting to fall apart. I remember driving to Bangor to invigilate an exam, and the exhaust nearly fell off. It started making an awful noise, but thankfully I made it to my destination. I called Dr G and told him I was too scared to drive home, so he and his dad sorted something out so I could drive Dr G's car home, and his dad drove my car to get fixed at a local garage.

For my birthday in 2018, Dr G surprised me by buying me a car. However, he didn't tell me as such. We just drove to the garage that the family used in Oswestry, so by the time I worked out where we were going, I'd guessed. I didn't know what to say. I was happy but shocked. No one had ever made that big a gesture to me before. He got it on a lease, so it worked out cheaper, and the idea was that I paid off the remaining balance in summer 2021.

My own car—I was ecstatic! It got scratched after just a few months, but it sort of came with the job. I used to give my student lifts when the weather was bad, but sometimes his stick would catch the paintwork on my car. At least I could still do my jobs independently, and now I didn't have to worry about the car falling apart from under me. My parents were upset, though. Why hadn't Dr G consulted them? What my mum hadn't told me was that she'd spent her inheritance from when her mum had died, on the car she gave to me. I felt sorry for that, but they had to understand that it wasn't viable to keep it anymore. Dr G and his family always used the same car dealer, so even though my dad has a special interest in cars, they already knew which model would be good, and I was happy with that.

Dr G then upgraded his car in January 2017. He wanted five doors ready for when the baby was born. The first night it was home, the door got scratched. We'd been to the Nintendo Switch premiere, and it was around 2 am when we arrived home and he parked slightly too close to the wall. My friend didn't realise. That car was cursed, or so he believed by the end.

In January 2018, we were in a car crash. It wasn't our fault, but we had to be towed the two hours home. We were filling the car with petrol at a supermarket forecourt. Dr G had just got back into the car, and before we knew it, we were shunted a foot forward as a car from behind slammed into the rear corner of our car and nearly plummeted through the front of the shop! It was shocking, but thankfully no one was injured. That same year at Christmas, he was in a local crash. A sheet of black ice was to blame, and another car slid into him. The second crash wasn't his fault. By Christmas 2019, he was in another local crash. Someone didn't see him when they were pulling out of a junction. It wasn't his fault. Dr G's car had to be towed away again. He'd had enough at that point.

In the new year, he decided to change his car again. He got the same model but upgraded it in February 2020. He barely used it before we went into lockdown, and I only managed to drive it once. A year later, he decided to get rid of his car altogether. He hadn't been anywhere. He'd been working at the dining table since March 2020. What a waste. He sold his car back to the dealer in February 2021, so we just had my car to share. Since lockdown ended, I seemed to go more places than he did. He did get his own car again in September 2021, thankfully.

My car has three stickers that make it mine. A golden Triforce from *Zelda*, a black squid from *Splatoon* and a Boo Ghost from the *Mario Series*. They've helped me out a few times. When I'm in an awkward silence somewhere, and a stranger spots my stickers, they strike up a conversation. A memorable incident was parking up to drop off my child at school. At the time, we had to go via the back gate due to Covid-19 restrictions. A man had a go at me for parking on his drive. I honestly didn't realise it was his drive, it was quite an open space, but I apologised anyway. He also triggered me. I had to pick up my child regardless, so I promised the man I'd be no more than five minutes. He reluctantly backed down. I picked up my child. I came back to the car, and he was stood outside still. My brain went into panic mode. To my surprise, he smiled, "Hey, I noticed the Triforce on the back of your car. I love *Zelda*!" Immediately, the anxiety lifted. He wasn't the enemy; he was a friendly face. We had a quick conversation about gaming and waved each other a good day before parting ways. We both left with a smile. Those three stickers were the first time I began to show more to the public world that I was an adult gamer.

LEARNING HOW TO ADULT

My twenty-first birthday was pretty lonely. Hardly anyone was around, and no one would come and visit me. My twentieth and twenty-first birthdays were the only birthdays I was single. I graduated from university the first time when I was twenty-one, and I stayed to do a part-time master's degree, so I graduated again at the age of twenty-three. I was married at twenty-six, and for most of my twenties, I was on zero-hour contracts.

After I rebelled against my parents' wishes of wanting me to do a PGCE, I had aspirations after my master's degree. I wanted to write music for film or video games. The more I progressed through my master's degree, the more I resented composing. I also took notes in a student's film music lectures and realised I didn't like the sound of that industry. I remember listening to an interview with a female composer based in Los Angeles. The line that stuck with me was, "If you're married, forget it. You'll be divorced in a few months." I was planning my wedding at the time. That was just awkward.

For video games music, I was told you had to know how to code. In my online PC gaming days, I'd run an IRC (Internet Relay Chat) channel and created a bot for it. I had also set up and run an active forum, learning a bit of HTML coding as I went along. Now they were talking C++ and JavaScript. It went straight over my head. I decided that I was way out of my depth for video games music.

I finished my master's degree not knowing what I wanted to do. For several years, I'd have my parents in one ear insisting I do the PGCE even though I had absolutely no interest in becoming a classroom teacher. Given my problems with anxiety, I wouldn't have lasted a day in that world. The kids would have made me cry on the first day! I was sad to leave my school initially, but that was because I was afraid of change, not because I was aspiring to be one of the teachers.

I started note taking while studying for my master's degree, which was my backup job until 2016. That was the year I turned thirty, so I guess it's safe to say I was basically a support worker in my twenties, except the eighteen months where I had the good office job, then the job from hell!

When I was twenty-four, I got engaged. It was an anxious time, but that year also had plenty of positives. There was the in-law family holiday, planning a wedding, I graduated from my master's degree—it was all looking up. I also passed my driving test that year. It was a big year for achievements.

At twenty-five, I was diagnosed with high blood pressure. That hit me like a ton of bricks. It was also the year I injured my back trying to do yoga and got whiplash from a car journey with my brother, as he'd not long passed his driving test. He didn't notice a stop sign until a motorbike went in front of him, and he jammed on the brakes. That was the start of my chronic back problems. At the time, I was fobbed off by the doctor. They tried to throw painkiller medication at me, but I refused. I wanted a long-term solution, not a quick fix. At the time, I didn't have the money to go to a private clinic. I sought help in 2014, which started as a regular massage, but by 2015 was a more hardcore deep tissue massage and the start of seeing a way out of the pain. The injuries ran deep and had years of stress and anxiety knots on top of them. My core muscles were shot, and my lower back was under a lot of stress as it was overcompensating. 2015 started the long road of trying to recover, right up until lockdown.

I set up my gaming community when I was twenty-six, and it will be ten years old later this year. When the rest of my life was rocky, the constant was my community that thrived out of nothing. I had created a great rapport with all the students I supported, and some even stayed in touch. That period of my employment ended with the sighted guide work, but by the age of twenty-nine, I was still deep in my anxiety bubble.

Two years of anxious wedding planning, then an anxious wedding, what was married life like after the wedding? It was okay, except for my mood swings. One thing I'd carried from my childhood, though, was my ability to write. The school may have thought my writing was mediocre, but my mum always said I wrote lovely letters. Pressured thank you cards were a thing when I was growing up too. I loved having occasional pen pals over the years, but eventually, they all dropped off. The latest pen pal was an old university friend that moved overseas, but she stopped writing by the time lockdown hit. There was the friend who lived up the road from me at my parents' that I wrote to in my first couple of years at university, but eventually, she stopped writing too.

I used to write to my nana, but because of illness, she was unable to write back. I still treasure the last ever text she sent to me, "yyggtff". She was trying to type thank you as I'd wished her a happy birthday. She died the week before my twenty-seventh birthday, less than two months later. It was bittersweet as she'd been able to see photos of me getting married, but she and my grampy never made it to the wedding the year before, as she'd just been diagnosed with cancer, and he had also been diagnosed with vascular dementia. I lost my final grandparent at the end of 2014. It's like I took it as a sign that starting 2015 with a funeral wasn't going to be a great year. It turned out to be one of the worst years of my life.

I did, however, put on a very successful event in mid-Wales with over eighty attendees in the middle of 2015. It was sensational, and that marked my twenty-ninth birthday. I also got a distinction on a Welsh exam that summer too.

I was then diagnosed with Generalised Anxiety Disorder when I was twenty-seven. I even got a free gym referral based on my anxiety diagnosis, but this didn't help with my mental state at all. However, it forced me to think about proper exercise for the first time in a while.

Basically, my twenties were emotional. I was low paid with jobless summers but had a year of decent jobs. I would have lots of mental ups and very low downs, but I also found my soulmate and married him. They weren't too bad really. And besides, if I hadn't had started that decade of my life by defying my parents' wishes, I'd have never met my soulmate.

In my young teens, and my journal, I wrote that I'd have a kid at thirty, and having already been married with my own house at twenty-six, it was an easy assumption for the outside world to assume. I figured my life would be sorted at thirty. However, I was still scared of everything, even though I'd ticked two out of three of those boxes. At least I had my diagnosis. I felt like I sort of knew what I was dealing with. Even though I'd had counselling and done a mindfulness course, I didn't really feel like I'd got anywhere, but I'd resigned to the fact that I was always going to be like that, and that was the hand I was dealt in life.

Upon finding out I was pregnant in the late summer, just after turning thirty, I signed up for some Cognitive Behavioural Therapy (CBT) to help with my anxiety. It ended up being focused entirely on my fear of being pregnant. It was purely coincidental timing-wise, as it just so happened that someone was training and looking for 'guinea pigs' to help her placement. It actually worked in that short space of time. During my pregnancy, I became complacent rather than anxious.

2017 hit its own obstacles. Having a baby is a life-changing thing, and it tests any relationship, no matter the situation. I was at high risk for post-natal depression but discharged because I had a good support network. My support network was indeed fantastic, but even with all the support in the world, when you've got an anxiety disorder, you can still feel anxious and sometimes lonely too. I tried to attend mum groups and joined apps on my phone. Most of the time, I got ghosted after the first meeting, which made me feel like a failure at making friends. I failed at breastfeeding. Then I failed at expressing milk. I didn't bond with my child for the first few months of his life. Thankfully, my supportive husband would remind me every so often that I was doing my best, and that's what mattered. I needed those words then. Mid-2017 until mid-2019 was basically survival mode.

We didn't get back into the bedroom stuff for the first six months. He didn't mind for the first few months, as we were sleep-deprived. Every moment of sleep mattered. After six months, we weren't as bad, so the expectation on his side returned. I was reluctant as I was still sleep-deprived, but I also felt like I had duties, so I just went through the motions over time. I was struggling with balancing everything as a working mum, but on reflection, I was also grateful that I only took two weeks off and not a whole year, as I wouldn't have coped with the big change from one mode to another.

In the early summer of 2016, I took on a side job. It was 0.07 of FTE (full-time equivalent), which meant that no one really wanted it, but it suited me perfectly. It was a way to stay as a staff member without actually being a proper member of staff. I was assistant to a professor, and my job was to transcribe things occasionally whilst helping with conferences and the webpage. The end of that job was the peak. My job was to organise an international conference.

In January 2018, we were in a car crash. I'm surprised we'd gone unscathed that long given that both of us had been driving while sleep-deprived at various points the last few months. It wasn't our fault, though. We were getting petrol, Dr G had just got into our car, and we were shunted forward as a car flew sideways past us and crashed into the bollard in front of the shop. A few seconds earlier meant the car would have struck Dr G before getting in the car. He could have been killed! We were an hour and a half away from home, and it took us a few hours to get home with our broken car on the back of a trailer. Mentally this threw me even further down. I struggled to cope with the shock and had a useless physiotherapist. I had chronic back pain anyway, so I couldn't tell the difference, but I was treated for whiplash with a TENS machine. When I returned to my sports lady, she told me the physiotherapist had made my back worse rather than better.

March 2018 was that aforementioned conference. I was still sleep-deprived, but for once, I had a tiny ounce of confidence, even though I was shaky and on edge for the whole thing. I managed to put on a front that saw me through. I was efficient, and the guests loved my customer service. I even took a visiting professor on a little tour of Anglesey the day after the conference had finished. I'd met the group at the pub the night before the two-day conference. I was nervous and shaky, but once we sat down and people started talking to me, I was a bit calmer then.

I mainly sat outside the room on the days of the conference, so I was able to spend some quiet time on my own, which was nice, even though I nearly nodded off quite a few times. The guests were happy with the food, and everyone was impressed with the efficiency and organisation of it all. I received a fancy bunch of flowers for my troubles, but that was it; the job ended there. I carried on helping Michael after that, so kept my links with the university. I was always used to having two or three jobs on the go. It was confusing for the taxman, but I loved the variety of my days and the fact I did contrasting things.

In August 2018, a close family friend passed away. I had to attend her funeral, as I wouldn't have missed it for anything. I was anxious all day, too nervous to speak to people I knew from childhood. I stuck by my brother and one other person all day, then became emotional at the bereaved husband when I had to leave. One memory that stuck in my mind was outside after the church service had concluded. I was chatting to an old family friend, and they asked what I did. I told them I ran a gaming community, and my dad, who was standing behind me, audibly tutted. I added loudly, "I must apologise for my dad. He obviously thinks my life is a joke." I already had plenty of self-doubt in my mind, but at that point, I was a piano teacher and was starting to get somewhere. My successful gaming community was six years old and going strong. At that moment, I showed a tiny bit of confidence standing up to my dad.

My mental health, in general, was a very rocky ride, and the first couple of years after I had my child were very unstable. Every few months or so, I felt my brain would shut down. When I got really anxious or stressed over a long period of time, I would slowly withdraw from everything around me and become emotionless or super emotional, non-physical and distant. This didn't go unnoticed by Dr G, but rather than approach me about it, he would become withdrawn too. Often it would go on for weeks, and we'd get more distant, until one day, I'd find the guts to say something, and it would all come out. It would only ever get talked about at 3 am when we both needed sleep. However, I was at the point where I couldn't sleep because I was too anxious. I later found out that he'd thought about leaving me a few times but had stayed for the baby. I was terrified. I knew it was bad, but I couldn't stop it from happening. It happened roughly every quarter. I'd get anxious about something, or there would be a major trigger, then the whole process would start again.

One night in late 2018, Dr G upped and left. I was stressed, but I had no idea what had caused him to leave. I called his dad in a panic, and his dad located him just down the road sat in his car. He'd got to the top of the hill in our village and pulled into a lay-by. He eventually came home, where I was worried sick! As it turned out, that time, it wasn't just about me; it was about everything in his life. He was lonely, and something one of our friends had said while gaming online, triggered him. He'd had enough but also didn't know what to do. We managed to sort it out, and I tried to be more mindful in general.

Christmas 2018 was lonely for both of us. We weren't really talking, but I had to sort the mess out before our New Year's Eve party. After finding the guts a couple of nights before, we managed to sort it out, but I was on edge for the whole of Christmas. 2019 was a bad year too. We were just about getting to the point of no longer being sleep-deprived. I would still shut down, but they were spaced out a bit more.

We went to a food festival in the summer of 2019, and

I was aware we were going through an episode again. I knew how to recognise them now, but I also didn't get any better at tackling them. He didn't like approaching me because I always became over-emotional, but we'd end up in a stalemate, which wasn't good for anyone. We barely talked during the festival. I tried to make it fun, but he just wasn't engaging. I started to recognise that his eyes would go stone cold; it wasn't just his physical distance. It was like he'd stare through me. It broke my heart. Of course, I got emotional. I still loved him with all my heart. However, in the depths of my anxiety, he felt ignored as I'd withdrawn yet again. We sorted it out with another late-night heart-to-heart, and I promised to try and change.

The last time it significantly happened was Christmas 2019, when it had been going on for about a month. I'd got stressed in the autumn and had been on edge ever since. I had survived on sugar for too long, and after my visit to the hospital in September, I was anxious about everything again. I knew I couldn't deal with it this time, but I also knew it was happening. It was absolute hell in my head. I was in the wrong, but it was also my mental health that was the issue. I hated using my mental health as an excuse, but I decided to make it my explanation. I went back to basics. When we first got together all those years ago, whenever we fell out, I'd write him an email to apologise or explain. I, therefore, wrote him a letter on Google. A full page and a bit of exactly why I'd been behaving like I had. I tried to deconstruct my thoughts in writing in the hope he could understand my anxiety disorder on a deeper level. I listed all my responsibilities: I was a working mum. I had a business, a job, a child. I was a wife, a sister, a daughter, a relative. I had to make sure we had things to eat, not to mention keeping the house in order. As well as remember to look after me on top of all that. I basically couldn't cope, so I put it all down—every single item. I was just about to share it one morning, and I'd just dropped off my child at nursery when I got a phone call. "I've been in a crash."

Thankfully, it was just down the road in the local town. He was at a junction, and the front side of his car was smashed. Someone had pulled out and hadn't seen him. It wasn't a highspeed crash, but it was enough that his car had to be towed away again. I had to take him to work in my car, which made me late for my Christmas do and even more anxious for everything else. That night I was determined to send the document. I just added a sentence on the bottom. '*Given what has happened today, it might be worth me asking if we could put things into perspective a bit?*'

Since that letter, we've not had another episode. The deeper understanding of my anxiety disorder and promising to communicate more gave me a new strength for our relationship. I also believe he knows how to communicate a lot more effectively too. We've grown together since then. I was thirty-three, and life was still far from sorted. I was very anxious and on edge every minute of every day. I didn't know what it was like not to be anxious or stressed anymore, but I thought I had to live with it. At least as a couple, we were sorted. We'd finally adjusted to being parents as well.

THE DIAGNOSES

I had asthma, hay fever and eczema as a child, which followed me into adulthood, though weirdly, I was on the strongest antihistamines before I had my child, but I don't need to take anything these days. I grew out of the asthma, and the eczema is kept at bay by my wonderful skincare products. The bigger diagnoses didn't happen until much later.

I'd moved house in 2012 and registered with a new doctor. They did a general health check, and she picked up the fact that my blood pressure seemed quite high. They wanted to double-check, so I was sent home with a twenty-four-hour blood pressure monitor. It was awful. I was really anxious but trying my best to keep calm. Every hour it would measure my blood pressure, and a couple of times, the cuff squeezed my arm so tight I thought I would be crushed, so my brain went into panic mode, and the blood pressure spiked. Then randomly, in the middle of the day, someone rang our doorbell, which made me jump, so it spiked then too. After I took it back to the nurse, she was shocked at how much it spiked. She muttered about how was I still alive? They wanted me to take medication to get it under control, but I was terrified of pills, as my mum always told me not to take them. However, a doctor stepped in and said they were trialling a new solution that involved training you to breathe deep. It used to be a fixed time, playing harp arpeggios in time to a deep inhale and exhale. I kept it going for a year until a fateful day in 2013 when I was helping Dr G with his office job, I nearly collapsed. I'd had a bad year mentally and was on edge all of the time. It had obviously become too much for me that day, so I ended up in the doctor's surgery in tears. I admitted defeat; I had to take the medication. Deep breathing just wasn't enough on its own. I was given beta blockers. It was only a minimal dosage, so I felt a little bit better about the prospect of having to take medication. The next day having to start the medication, I was shaking. I didn't want to take them, and I burst into tears again. I was a failure, and I couldn't look after myself. I was now going to be stuck on medication for life.

I found out the condition was hereditary, but my mum said her side had never experienced high blood pressure. I asked my dad, and he said neither had they, but it had to be one of them, so that didn't make sense. I later found out that it was my dad's side. All his siblings had suffered with high blood pressure at some point. My aunt had suffered from it when she was pregnant, my uncle currently had it, and my younger aunt had experienced it in the past too. The doctor's advice was useless. I remember echoes of the nurse tutting and saying, "You're so young," whilst glancing at the advice leaflets. All the leaflets assumed the patient was middle-aged or older, obese and inactive, or eating too much salt. I was twenty-five, didn't eat salt, was fairly active and definitely not obese.

Later in 2013, we sorted out life insurance, and blood pressure was an issue on the acceptance side, so they sent someone over to check. On the day, my blood pressure decided to co-operate, so I passed the test. I'll always wonder how my body managed to do that, considering I was so convinced I wouldn't be accepted.

I was on the minimal dose of beta blockers until 2015 when I had to double my dose. I had more stress because of the nightmare office job I had at the time. By the time I was pregnant towards the end of 2016, I had to change from beta blockers to antihypertensives. Tablets went from one a day to three times a day—it was hell. The new medication didn't work, and my blood pressure kept spiking. However, they wouldn't do anything about it because when I was most rested, it was technically fine. I was at high risk for pre-eclampsia, and despite numerous extra visits to the hospital, the blood pressure 'behaved' in the end.

I had to wait until I'd finished expressing milk in September 2017 before I could go back on beta blockers. I was so relieved. However, the bad news was I had to go back on the higher dose again. What I didn't realise was that I had slowly gained weight. I was categorically obese already, but I felt it this time. It was starting to get me down, my anxiety was sky high, but I also couldn't stop eating sugar. I needed it to keep awake. It sort of worked until I ended up in hospital in 2019. In 2020, I lost most of the weight and was finally in a place where I was happy. But it wasn't until February 2021 I was finally able to reduce my dose back to what it was when I was first diagnosed nine years ago.

I believe I've had General Anxiety Disorder since I was thirteen years old. I was fortunate that I kept a diary throughout my teenage years every single day. I put down my feelings and what I had been doing. It was also the age I got my first boyfriend, Henry. It details how I got myself into knots during my GCSE year, being bullied consistently, and the negativity at home. It all accumulated in me being scared of pretty much everything. Heart palpitations and heart in mouth were quite familiar feelings, as well as feeling sick, crying often and shaking. Most of the time, I was a silly little girl or was told to snap out of it. It was considered a normal part of growing up, except it wasn't. No one else seemed to get that worked up about stuff.

It continued well into later teenage life and adulthood. Everything I did had anxiety running through it. Being afraid of change meant that I was stuck in zero-hours contracts for years, unable to find a job or career I actually wanted: no direction, no hopes, no goals, nothing. However, I was a super empath too, and I was generally great at holding down relationships. So despite all the failures at job, career, and life in general, I managed to find my soulmate and marry him.

It was 2009, the first time the anxiety became sky high. I didn't realise, but I'd had the Depo-Provera contraceptive injection and hadn't thought about the side effects. My body went stiffer over time, and I started getting paranoid that the contraceptive was affecting my bones. After I cancelled the appointments, I realised possible side effects could cause osteoporosis and exacerbate mental health issues. My anxiety went into overdrive. I was finishing my master's degree and struggling. At worst, I wouldn't even leave the house. I was afraid of people looking at me.

After I stopped and recovered from the effects of the contraceptive, things got a bit better, but I never stopped feeling on edge. Twenty-four hours a day, seven days a week on edge, I was always worrying about something and catastrophising. I survived the wedding, the planning, the diagnosis of high blood pressure, but at the point, I was resigned to the medication for life. I realised I needed proper help. In early 2013 I signed up for an eight-week mindfulness course and booked a doctor's appointment. The course was interesting, but it finished just as my nana died, so I was emotional. When we did the meditation sessions, I knew I'd relaxed when I'd fall asleep, but then I felt like I'd failed because I fell asleep.

The doctor listened to my emotional pleas and diagnosed me with generalised anxiety disorder. Why am I scared of everything? Of nothing specific? Just always on edge, nervous, unsettled and not being able to think straight. I struggle to sleep properly. The line that rings in my head over many years since beginner's Welsh classes is, "What do you do to relax?" I never had the answer, as I couldn't identify what being relaxed actually was. It was only towards the end of 2021 I started to discover what it felt like to no longer be on edge all the time.

DWI'N DYSGU CYMRAEG
"I'm Learning Welsh"

When I started dating Dr G, even though he was a learner himself, he felt it was really important for me to learn Welsh if I was going to stick around. Many years later, we found it was hilarious when the *Cards Against Humanity* craze happened. The card which said '... *pronouncing all the names of Northern Welsh Towns*' had him and I exchanging side glances with a smirk every time it appeared. His parents still lived on the east side of North Wales, so we used to go and visit them, and he would pronounce every single town we went through and would challenge me to pronounce them too. It was annoying at the time, but it proved invaluable in future years for work.

In 2008, I participated in the Welsh Learners Summer School. I was able to find the time in between my shifts at the supermarket. I was anxious, I hated group work, but I tried my best. I enjoyed the long walk between the house and the class while the weather was nice. I made a couple of friends, but due to my fear of messaging people, we lost touch almost as soon as the classes had finished. The only exception was the one person I liked but was too scared to talk to in the actual classes, Emily. We connected after the classes had finished. We were both shy, but we had a lot in common. She joined the choir I was singing in, and we used to meet up regularly for drinks or food. The classes were taught by repetition, which was great, but it didn't really stick after I left as I didn't have the confidence to practice in the groups we were in, let alone outside.

I did the same course again, but as a note taker for my student, Miles. This time the words stuck. It was a completely different approach to learning. The tutor wasn't keen as I don't think she liked the idea of extra work, but I was ready and willing. I had to take notes in English, Welsh and phonetics. I hadn't learnt the official phonetic alphabet, so I made them up, but Miles loved it, and we learned together. After taking the first course, I followed up a couple of years later. When you held a staff position at the university, Welsh classes were free—it was a no brainer.

I signed up straight away, and I got a bit carried away, signing up for both lunchtime and evening classes. The lunchtime classes were a lot slower paced, so I was getting bored, even though the tutors were lovely. I ended up just doing the evening classes. Monday was usually fine, but Thursday, I was tired from all the hours I'd worked in the office job and would often start nodding off. I would always get embarrassed, but I couldn't help it either. I pushed through, and despite being in the middle of the job from hell at the time, I was determined for it not to impact my ability to function. I ended up getting a distinction for the exam that summer, despite being one of the most stressful weeks of my life.

I carried on studying, but I ended up skipping a class as my existing one was unable to continue due to a lack of numbers. I didn't mind at first. It was ok, and I was just about able to keep up. I was always scared of group work, so I just sat there and hoped a nice person would come and work with me. Most of the time, they did, but occasionally I'd end up working with the tutor because I was on my own. Both Dr G and his sister were in the same class, but we purposely distanced ourselves because we could practice at home if we really wanted to. This inevitably didn't happen because I was too anxious to try.

I passed the next exam. There was no distinction this time, just a pass, but I enjoyed the speaking test even though initially I dreaded it. Being able to talk about one of my passions helped. During that year, I won a writing competition for the learners' Eisteddfod. It was pinned back to me, but I also submitted it with a fake name, as I was too shy to get myself out there and didn't think it was any good. I was elated that someone thought different! I won a book token for my troubles, which I spent on Welsh children's stories, ironically just a year before I knew I was going to have a child.

The following year didn't go so well, though. We were now on the 'A' level equivalent when I found out I was pregnant but didn't want to tell anyone and was struggling to stay alert in the classes. I was dozing off regularly, and at the pace it was now, I couldn't keep up. I emailed the tutor and apologised that I had to give up because I just found it too hard. I told him about my pregnancy, but I didn't want to tell the rest of the class. My anxiety made me scared of being pregnant, so the fewer people that knew, the better.

I never returned to Welsh classes, but my child is bilingual, so I'm always listening to or reading Welsh somewhere.

MY SOULMATE FOUND ME

When I met my soulmate, Dr G, in the same week as Liam, it was at a training lunch for my new zero-hours contracted job as a note taker. Romance in that setting was definitely unique, but it also wasn't love at first sight. I'd just started dating Liam, so I wasn't looking for anyone else, but Dr G was. He started chatting to me, which I was glad of because, being socially awkward, I wouldn't approach anyone myself.

I forgot about Dr G completely after that first meeting. When we met again, I pretended to remember him. One thing changed this time, we went into town together, and he gave me an Aero Bubble in HMV. I certainly remembered him after that. He tracked my email address down on the university system and we had a good dialogue over email for the first few months. Eventually, we met for a hot chocolate and started talking properly. I discovered he was in his mid-twenties and loved *Mario Kart.* I'd loved that game as a child but had almost forgotten about it until the end of my third year, when I was reconciled with my N64.

In November 2007, Dr G had a voucher for a lunch deal at a local tapas bar. He suggested I use it with a friend, but I knew Liam wasn't into that kind of food. It turned out Dr G was planning on going all along, with the intention of asking me out. At the point of meeting, he realised I already had a boyfriend, because that's all I talked about. Over the next couple of months, we kept regular email contact. I started joining him and his housemate, Ed, for poker nights, and we started to get to know each other.

Two incidents happened in those three months. The first one was when a friend dared me to audition for a solo in the choir. I was shaky, but I did it. Alas, I didn't get the part and was told my voice was too weak. I went home to Liam, who said, "Oh, did that mean you were crap?" I was shocked! Surely a boyfriend is supposed to be supportive. Meanwhile, Dr G told me via email that he was proud of me for trying.

The second incident was in early December. It was the Music Society Christmas Concert. I had been trying to persuade Liam to come along after he'd recently revealed that he didn't like music. I was nervous and felt like I needed moral support, but he wouldn't budge, despite one of his best friends also being in the choir. Walking down to the venue, his friend agreed with me that he should have come to support me. I arrived at the venue and bumped into Dr G. He'd come to support me. I was so touched; it was at that point I realised I was with the wrong guy.

Consequently, Liam was slipping down my priority list. That Christmas, just before the holidays, I stayed over at Dr G's house instead of spending time with my actual boyfriend. Liam had let me down too many times at that point, and although I felt guilty, I did it anyway. Dr G and I made a giant Jaffa cake as a present for one of his friends. He made us tea, and we watched a film. He slept on the sofa so I could have the bed. All above board. Except for the bit when he said he liked me 'more than a friend'.

Over Christmas, I could only describe it as 'emotional limbo'. I decided I'd see what Liam had bought me for Christmas and then decide what to do. It was honestly the worst Christmas present I could have hoped for, and I'd put a lot of effort into his, having bought it a few months earlier, when the relationship was a lot more optimistic. In return, I received a DVD I already had and a generic CD of classical music. The worst bit was that had he taken the time to get to know me, he'd have realised I wasn't even that into classical music at the time. I was gutted but also relieved, as that made the decision for me.

I hated making big decisions and tended to just fall into them so I could avoid the anxiety that inevitably hit me like a ton of bricks. This time I had to do it, so being that I learnt it was bad manners to dump someone via text, I made sure I did it face to face. I wimped out halfway through, though and told Liam a lie. I said I was dumping him because I needed to focus on my studies, but I was too scared to tell him outright that I thought I'd already found my soulmate. Just three days later, Dr G and I were an item. Dr G was indeed my soulmate, and it only took him a week to tell me he was in love with me. The feeling was mutual, and things had never felt so right.

I'd long believed that in order to build a successful relationship, a couple should be at least friends first, if not best friends. Henry was my best friend first. Jonesy was my best friend first. The relationships both lasted approximately three years each, so I had to be doing something right. Liam was the only one I'd dated where I didn't technically know him beforehand, and that was the only one that lasted a short time of three months. Dr G and I were close friends first. Maybe we were even best friends, but we'd only known each other for four months. Surely that was too brief to be considered best friends, but we'd talked a lot in those short months. Due to the many emails and conversations, it felt like I'd known him forever.

I was scared to get in too deep after Jonesy had well and truly broken my heart, but I couldn't help who I fell in love with either. Dr G was 'the one', and I knew it. The rocky start showed us all sides of each other: my anxiety, his stresses, the conflict about housework and food. The food became such an issue before we moved in together that I wrote him a checklist of vegetables that he had to tick to say what he was willing to eat. We used to write each other poetry for Christmas, birthdays and Valentine's Day; it was magical.

We stood by each other through thick and thin and came out of the other side with the sunshine. Over the hill, it was shining bright, and we had the rest of our future to look forward to. Everything was pretty rosy, except the odd occasion. Whenever we fell out, we didn't row, he would go silent, and I would become super anxious. The only way I could break the silence was to write him a letter or email, so that's what I did. Over the years, this proved very useful, as I've always been a lot more articulate with writing than saying things out loud. It has helped us process many arguments over the years, and I've been able to explain myself so that he's able to communicate properly with me. Usually, it was him who had got his back up, but I struggled to communicate initially, as every time I tried to talk about subjects close to my heart, I would shake and get over-emotional.

Looking back, we were at one of his family friends' weddings in 2009. It was a really hot day, and I was socially anxious. I tried my best to enjoy it and fit in. All the ladies were wearing dresses, but I didn't have the confidence to wear one myself, so I turned up in black trousers and a baggy floral top that I didn't really care for. The menu was excellent. In fact, it was my taste, so I ended up eating everyone's duck starters because no one liked it. Dr G didn't even like the chicken for his main course, so he was pretty hungry all day until the evening. Everything was running late, so there was a lot of time waiting around, and because it was so hot, all I could think about was whether I was perspiring. The night wasn't much better. I wasn't used to sleeping away, and due to the duvet being filled with feathers, I was allergic to it. I didn't think to check about the feathers until I woke up at six the next morning, unable to breathe. The evening stuck in my head because I stayed by the same table all night. Neither of us would dance. Dr G casually mentioned that we should start thinking about 'this' soon. Personally, the thought had never crossed my mind. We hadn't been together that long, and I was only twenty-two.

A few months later, Dr G and I attended a staff ball at the university. I was socially anxious again, and I hardly talked to anyone unless they talked to me. I swear Dr G got tipsy as he mentioned engagement again, and I shrugged it off. Things went a bit weird that night as I was anxious and confused about what he'd said but didn't want to bring the subject back up.

A year later, we were engaged. He proposed by a riverside, except he didn't. Personality-wise, we were both very much introverts, shy and rubbish at talking about big life things, so it's no wonder he bottled it on the day. He 'tested' the water in the early summer and invited me on my first family holiday. Five of us went to Fuerteventura, and it was a great week, but I was terrified of being ill. What I didn't realise, until after we came home, was that my body didn't like the climate of Fuerteventura, so I took one dip in the swimming pool and got a nosebleed for the rest of the week. I remember spending half the time with tissue stuffed up my nose and the other times putting sugar up it.

I managed until we arrived at the airport. We were fortunate that we could use the fast lane because his mum was using a stick due to a recent operation. I always became super anxious at airports after the trip to the Netherlands in 2004. He made a joke that I looked like a terrorist! This made me go into panic mode, and I nearly cried and vomited! We survived, but then on the way back, I was anxious because the plane was delayed, and we got back in the middle of the night. Overall, we enjoyed the holiday, and it was great to experience a different way of life.

A month or so later, we were engaged. We were staying at his parents' house, and he'd planned a day out using the Ffestiniog Railway. On our way out, his dad said, "Hope you have a good visit to the grave." Dr G shushed him and hurried us out of the door. We went on the railway to

Beddgelert (hence the grave reference), and on the way, he asked if I'd like a snack. When we found out there were only gluten-free coconut macaroons, I declined. Before I knew it, he'd come back with a macaroon, and I was confused, but I said nothing and reluctantly ate it. At that point, I twigged that he was particularly nervous about something.

We went to the riverside, and he was supposed to propose to me there. He didn't have a ring, and he was so nervous he couldn't get his words out. He asked, "Do you see us as a permanent couple?" I couldn't help but laugh, albeit nervously. "Do you mean, like, a wedding?" I asked quietly. He nodded. "Ok then," I replied. "But not for two years, right?" Two years because then I might be mentally prepared? I don't know, but I knew I wasn't quite ready to be married, even though I knew I wanted to marry him.

The couple whose wedding we'd attended in 2009 were still just about in the picture. We'd been around to their house for a family party, and I remember chatting to the wife in her kitchen. She was still gushing about her wedding and commented that I was welcome to copy anything from her ideas because hers was so remarkable. Meanwhile, I was thinking to myself that it was the most generic wedding I'd ever been to, and I planned on putting a much more personal touch on mine. I think I replied awkwardly with a smile and a nod, but a side glance at Dr G, which I think she might have caught. We left theirs, and nothing was said after that.

I was planning my wedding, and I wanted to do as much of it myself as I possibly could. I was aware we were on a budget but also wanted to make it personal and quirky. I created all the stationery myself, and I made my own centrepieces. I asked my mum to make a cake with stars that had eyes and decided on a starry night theme with crystals. Quite a few relatives tried to shape the day before I'd even considered anything.

The major problem was children. Both sides wanted children to be invited, but I didn't. It was my day, and the only children I knew were distant relatives. I had no nieces or nephews, nor did I have my own children, so it was a no-brainer as far as I was concerned. My parents respected the decision, but I think I must have squeaked when I told them, afraid of repercussions! Before I knew it, the mother-in-law had invited her friend Stella's granddaughter to be my flower girl. As soon as I heard, my heart leapt into my mouth. Crap! What do I do now? The girl would be gutted if I told her no, but there's no way I was having children at my wedding. Dr G told me he'd sort it, so he had a word with his mum, and his mum had to uninvite the flower girl. She respected our decision and did it, but the backlash was beyond anything I imagined.

The next thing I knew, Stella was accusing my mother-in-law of all sorts. She lashed out at Dr G and told him I was a manipulative cow, and he should avoid me at all costs. I didn't know what to think, but I also knew that both Dr G and his family knew me better than that. I was simply too anxious to be manipulative. The fallout concluded when they cut all contact. Initially, the mother-in-law was upset, but over time we came to realise a few things about the other woman. They'd been friends for many years, but Stella had always been controlling. She liked getting her own way, and when she didn't, she'd throw her toys out of the pram. The only difference was, this time, there was no battle to win. It was our wedding, not hers. We stuck to our guns. Her whole family cut contact, which was the last we ever heard of them.

At the start of the planning, I struggled to get my views across, but at least I had Dr G in my corner. He let me plan the wedding but would tell me if he didn't like something, which was fair. I think his only opinion at the start was he didn't want pink, which suited me because I hated the colour. I chose my colours first. I started with burgundy but realised it clashed with what I wanted to do. Secondly, I went with purple, but Dr G wasn't sure. I ended up settling on cobalt blue. Eventually, the theme became A Late Summer Starry Night —not too dark blue, but with plenty of sparkles!

I let the mothers choose my dress, but I picked my dream bridesmaids' dresses. We forgot about my old school friend Ian when hiring the suits, so he ended up with just a cravat. Thankfully, he didn't seem to mind, and his suit blended in fine anyway. Contact between the venue and other contributors were always anxiety-filled for me. I wouldn't pick up the phone unless I had to, did everything via email, and was simply too scared to chase people up if they took longer to reply.

By the end of the planning, I'd ordered two tiaras, but the poor shop went out of business halfway through, so I only had half of what I hoped for, but one was better than nothing. The makeup lady left the castle venue and was replaced, which triggered me because I was still afraid of strangers. The stationery wasn't too bad, but I did get stuck with ideas, so Emily's boyfriend's mum offered to help who handily ran a craft shop on Anglesey. One day we drove up there, and she tried out a few ideas with me, and I left full of all the creative ideas I needed to finish the rest of it.

Music was inevitably the most important bit. I worried about it for ages and decided to arrange a piece from the *Super Mario Galaxy* series for harp, flute and clarinet. I plucked up the courage to ask students to help me out, but the clarinettist was a bit demanding and caused me to panic on the day by asking me questions I didn't know the answer to. They did all turn up, at least. Everything came together quite nicely; two years to plan was perfect.

In the July, I had my hen party. I tried to invite quite a few people, but everyone turned me down. It ended up with six of us: the mums, the sister-in-law, my two bridesmaids and me. I planned chocolate making and a spa day with an overnight stay. It was lovely, but the venue hadn't told me there was a wedding happening at the same time, so we got closed off and could only use the little bar in a certain part of the hotel. I was too scared to complain, and when the bar staff claimed not to know how to make cocktails, I was gutted, but again too scared to complain. The meal was lovely, though, and the overall experience was great until I cut my toe open the next morning whilst having a dip. To top that off, both mothers were sick. Only four of us made it to breakfast, and then we made a hasty exit.

August was the month of the wedding, and so many things went wrong. We were both stressed, and people were arguing, but we made it. We'd made a weekend out of it, so I didn't have to panic about everything just on the day. My guys stayed in a townhouse, and his guys stayed in the castle venue. It was lovely. The day before, the groomsmen and bridesmaids were up and joined us for a spa in the castle. It was fun, despite Dr G flooding the hot tub room just as the member of staff was about to show around a potential client. That night we had a buffet tea for anyone who'd arrived the night before to join us. It was perfect, except for my anxiety.

After the food, I called a meeting for all of the immediate wedding party to go through the arrangements for the following day. I was shaking throughout. My dad commented that it was like military precision. It was supposed to be a compliment, but in my head, I knew that if I didn't do it this detailed, my mind would go into meltdown!

I was supposed to sing a song I'd written for Dr G. The piano in the house we were staying in was out of tune, so I'd panicked earlier in the day. My in-laws kindly brought up my digital keyboard but forgot the music stand, so I had a complete meltdown and bottled it completely. However, I did create a physical gift for him too, which I'd accidentally left with his mum in the castle. In the summer, I'd had a rare bout of confidence and booked myself for a boudoir shoot. I knew she'd made me look stunning, and I couldn't believe that with a bit of makeup, I could look that good. Of course, it was edited, but I thought that was it. I had confidence!

We parted ways for the night, and he locked himself in the bathroom of the room he was sharing with one of his best men, and he made the mistake of texting me just before going to sleep to say, 'We need to talk.' That text sent me into a wild panic, but it was midnight, and the rest of my house was already in bed and probably asleep. He'd also switched off his phone and gone to sleep, leaving me to have an anxiety attack in the dark, on my own. I was too scared that I'd wake someone up, so I hid but didn't sleep a wink that night.

I attended my wedding with no sleep. Thankfully, he was up at 7 am, so I texted, 'WHAT DO YOU MEAN?!!!!' He replied as if nothing had happened with something like, 'I just wanted to say I was speechless, it was amazing, and I'm so proud of you! Thank you.' I breathed a sigh of relief, but my mindset for the day was mush. I was on edge all day and even though it honestly was one of the best days of my life, I noticed every little detail that went wrong.

The day started on the wrong footing when the videographer started recording. He was a family friend who'd only done Romany weddings before. He started the day off by filming the wrong wedding guests! There were two weddings in the same venue that day. He was unable to edit the video properly to fix the music problems, so I ended up being upset about that but too afraid to say anything.

I'd trusted my brother with the sound check, which didn't seem to happen because I ended up walking out of the ceremony to near silence as far as the music was concerned. It was so quiet it was drowned out completely by clapping. I'd picked the end credits from *Super Mario Galaxy*, and it was supposed to be a big statement piece. I was gutted. The music woes didn't end there.

The ushers gave the wrong people the Orders of the Day. I'd only produced enough for one between two people, but we had 'Calon Lân', a traditional Welsh song, before the cutting of the cake. If it had been one per couple as expected, everyone would have had the words. It turned out that the ones who knew the tune didn't have access to the words. To make matters worse, the CD player was too quiet in the room. I was singing in tune, the in-laws were out of tune, and there was an awkward silence from the guests. I could feel myself going bright red throughout the song.

It wasn't just about the music, though. Plenty of other disasters happened. I asked my sister-in-law and brother to be our witnesses but realised that I'd forgotten to request official photos with them. The photographer was fantastic, but at the end of the day, he could only take photographs of what he knew about. Due to being taken away from the main reception area to have photos taken, I missed the entire musical performance my harpist performed. After the 'Calon Lân' fiasco, I was so anxious at the wedding breakfast. When Dr G did the 'real proposal' in his speech, I became so emotional I answered him short and went bright red.

I'd been on a gluten-free diet for a few years by the time I got married, so I'd sorted the menu out with the venue. The choice was roast beef or vegetarian ratatouille. I loved the sound of ratatouille, so I chose that for myself but marked myself as gluten-free. The venue wouldn't tell me what alternative they'd found for me. Without any warning, they served me mushroom risotto. I was not a fan of risotto or mushrooms, so I took one mouthful and decided I didn't like it. To make matters worse, my mum put in what she thought was a gluten-free brownie for my dessert, so I didn't miss out on the wedding cake, which was served as dessert to the rest of the guests. However, she managed to mistake organic for gluten-free.

As a consequence of hardly eating anything at the breakfast, I managed to get drunk for the first time. My friend, Steph, had made it over to my wedding and had bought me a big glass of Sex on the Beach as I'd told her it was my favourite cocktail. I got social anxiety at my own wedding by the evening and ended up sitting at the same table all night. I was also a bit zoned out and started telling random relatives passing by that I loved certain songs. The food for the buffet wasn't great either. I tried to eat but came across what I believed to be pickled cauliflower; I'd never heard of that before, and no one touched it. We finished the night in a close family circle, swaying along to Green Day's 'Time of your Life'. I always said that no matter who I married, that had to be the last song.

We didn't even make it to bed between the last song and the hotel room without something going wrong. I was a bit drunk, and we'd reached the outside of our hotel room door, scrambling to find the key. The couple in the room next door started shouting at us to be quiet. I was mortified! The next morning, they apologised when they realised it was us.

The final disaster was my poor wedding shoes. I'd bought Rainbow Club shoes as they were recommended by other brides on a forum I was part of and had them dyed electric blue. When my wedding day was over, they were anything but blue! Brown, green, scuffed ivory as the dye had run out of the shoes because the ground was wet where we'd had most of the photographs taken. I had to be reminded to be grateful that it hadn't rained on our actual wedding day.

A vast amount of things went wrong that day, yet family members would come to me and say what a perfect day it was. We also felt a sense of achievement. The groomsmen, bridesmaids and ourselves managed to have a Mario Kart DS time trial in one of the groomsmen's hotel rooms. I was so afraid of judgement before the day that I'd hidden it from the 'grown-ups' and the friends who weren't gamers. The photographer knew and took pictures, so we have the memories to keep forever.

I also forgot to thank most of the service people afterwards. I let too much time pass before I realised, and then I felt too awkward. I really did appreciate everyone, but I always felt guilty that I'd never let them know.

The biggest takeaway from my wedding day and the planning leading up to it was telling myself that if I could plan a wedding, I could plan anything! Of course, lots of things did go right. It was such a good day that relatives talked about it for years after, and every time I saw them would say how much they'd love to do it again.

FRIENDSHIPS

I wasn't bad at making friends as a kid at primary school. I had a few here and there, but never a large amount. I remember making my first best friend in year three—George. He was the one I used to do everything with, but when we moved up a year, he skipped to year five. I was left in year four, so we grew distant, and then I ended up with a different set of friends by year six. I think I stopped having best friends after about year four when a girl who used to go around with me, but we were both bullied. Back then, we fought back, and it didn't bother us. The memory that sticks is when a lad called us 'wet', and we retorted with 'dry' and then fell about giggling. I lost touch with her, though, as her family moved away, and we weren't allowed to write to each other.

For the rest of primary school, I was in a group, so didn't have a best friend. I just used to hang on to their every word to try and fit in. In secondary school, I always seemed to be the third wheel. I never had an actual best friend throughout the rest of my school life. There were a few people I could call friends, and I thought I had a best friend between years seven and eight, but I remember her one day falling out with me because she said I was too annoying. There were two girls who were each other's best friends, who took me on board and let me hang out with them, but as we got put into sets, we drifted apart because I was in the higher while they were in the lower.

My first boyfriend, Henry, was my best friend before we started dating, but he also had a best friend, so again, I was the third wheel. When we became a couple, the other guy used to get jealous, so Henry's best friend and I had a very rocky relationship until we left school.

One girl looked out for me for her entire five years at secondary school, but she was never really a best friend. Steph had loads of friends, but she also caught the school bus with me. I couldn't help but think she just felt sorry for me. She's one of the few school friends I still vaguely keep in touch with. I also had a best school bus friend, Holly, who was a couple of years younger than me. By the time I ended up at the front of the bus, I eventually found someone to sit next to, so we'd save each other a seat. When I started sixth form, she was getting a different bus. I remember she was vegetarian, as she used to show me when she had fake bacon as she found it funny. Later, when she got a different bus, I had a fellow sixth-former, Lucy, who got the same bus, so I had a buddy again.

There was a girl in my form throughout who was a bit odd. She had a reputation with the boys but also wasn't one of the popular girls. We only really got to know each other towards sixth form, and she became part of the group of eight friends. She never stuck up for me and would always flirt with my boyfriend. On reflection in later life, I wondered whether she'd befriended me to try and steal him. It never worked, though. She wasn't his type.

However, that group of eight gave me security. I mention in the 'Invisible Target' chapter that I was always a bit of an outcast because it ended up having my ex, Henry, in it. It also had Lucy. She was a Mosher. I loved how she was so sure of herself, so I tried to copy her look and started dressing all in black with accents of pink. I wore the rubber bracelets and bike chains up my arms and again tried to fit in, but this time with a slightly alternative look.

Within that group of eight was my oldest friend, Tom, who I'd known since I was two or three. We had fun, but I wasn't his best friend as he was very popular. He also accidentally punched me on the nose once and probably caused me to be prone to nosebleeds for the next few years. He played the saxophone, and I played the piano, so we used to spend our free periods together in the school hall, me accompanying his diverse repertoire!

I was with Jonesy by then. Like Henry, he was also my best friend before I dated him. There was always a bit of tension when he was involved because that larger friendship group sided with Henry when we split up, even though they tried to be neutral. My anxiety often told me they didn't like me because of what I'd done and were just putting up with me because they had to. I also remember there was a lone guy who was in Jonesy's music classes. I got to know Ian, but mainly we'd be taking the mick out of each other or just downright insulting each other! I always seemed to get the upper hand as I used to call him a name that he couldn't spell, so he couldn't look it up to find out what it meant. That carried on into my university years. Funnily enough, Ian was the one I stayed in touch with, whereas the larger group I didn't. Being scared of phones and everyone using texts/phone and letters being outdated, I couldn't keep up. As time passed, they became strangers. I didn't drink, and they used to go on nights out without me. It probably didn't help.

Ian helped me through life when I split up with Jonesy while I was at university. We used to chat on MSN, and he even joined the online PC game I'd been sucked into. At one point, I thought he had a crush on me, but my gaydar was awful. He was telling me all about his flatmate, and I didn't realise that was his crush until much later. I was a bit desperate for attention but also too anxious to chase it. I had a crush on two boys at university as well, but they never found out because I was too terrified to say anything.

Ian stuck by me, and we're still very much in touch now. We probably bonded initially by bashing Jonesy after he and I split up, but once I got that out of my system, we met up once or twice a year. He was the only person from home who came to visit me on location in Bangor, and he didn't mind that I was often too anxious to travel to him. When I went home during the holidays, we'd try to meet at the cinema in the city centre, which became a mini tradition. I nearly lost him for good in my third year, though. We'd gone for a walk, and he had only brought one pair of trousers with him. What I wasn't expecting was the cross-country path being muddy, so he lost his temper in the middle of the field and said he wasn't going to visit again! The grudge didn't stay long, and he started visiting again when he heard about my new boyfriend, Dr G. So he's now a mutual friend of ours and visits when he's able to get time off work. There was a point a couple of years into my relationship with Dr G when I suffered from a very low point with my mental health. Ian's insults were grinding me down, so I eventually called him out and we called a truce and promised never to do it again.

My first and second years at university were mainly me either being a hermit or just an outcast. The tutors had their favourites—particularly the guy who ran the main orchestra. I felt that he didn't like me, so I distanced myself. I got ignored often and would sit in the breaks of rehearsals on my own, staring at the floor because I was too scared to talk to people. This happened for quite a few years. I joined the society orchestra after dropping out of the first orchestra halfway through my first year. It was nothing like the youth orchestra from back home. There was one friend who stuck by me in my first year, but she dropped out halfway through second year. On reflection, she was always getting drunk and tried to get me to watch horror movies, so she perhaps wasn't the best kind of friend to have, but then any friend was a good friend, as I was pretty lonely.

There was one other person who stuck by me throughout my undergraduate life, Clare. She helped me join the initial societies, tried to include me in things, and we kept in touch beyond university too. She was even a bridesmaid at my wedding. There was also a boy who used to sit in corners at parties and stare at the floor with me. We didn't really stay in touch, simply because I was too scared to message him. There were other memories of passing friends, but none of them stuck. There were valuable lessons I learned many years later. My conclusion about university life was that I was always an outcast. I also realised in time that a lot of people I wished I could have connected with were also anxious, so we were nothing more than passing ships in the wind.

By the time I started my master's degree, I'd met Liam, as well as Dr G. Back then, I didn't really have any friends left. There was a small handful of us who stayed on for the master's degree from the undergraduate degree. The confident students got to know the lecturers and made friends with everyone. The shy ones withdrew into themselves.

At the beginning, I was friends with Liam's housemates. They'd invite me to parties and gaming sessions, and I tried to enjoy them as best I could. The people were great, but parties revolved around drinking, and of course, I never quite fitted in because I didn't really drink. When I split up with Liam, the friends went with him, so those brief friendships only lasted three months—back to square one. Dr G had a couple of long-distance friends and his housemate, Ed. I got to know Ed, and we got along well, but we also barely had anything in common other than our love of Nintendo and Poker. He was a gym nut, and I did try and copy him for a bit, but at that point, I didn't really have the motivation to stay consistent, so I was one of those people who signed up to the gym, then stopped going after a month.

I got along with Dr G's long-distance friends when they visited. We could chat for ages, and I felt like I was one of them. However, because they weren't local, those occasions were rare. I didn't really have any local friends for quite a long time. I had people to chat to, but in essence, I was too shy to talk to them consistently in a way that you would to form relationships, so I just drifted.

I had a couple of friends. Emily was really shy, and Rachel was outgoing but ridiculously unreliable for timekeeping. For my birthday in 2008, I invited six random friends to my birthday meal. Most of them had never met each other. Later, someone pointed out that you don't mix friendship groups, but since I didn't have a group to speak of, I'd thought nothing of it. Conversations were a bit awkward that night, but we survived.

Rachel was the one that stuck around, though. She lived in a house behind my favourite coffee shop, and we would try to meet for coffee or lunch semi-regularly. She was always super late. Not just ten minutes here or there, but even up to an hour and a half late! Most people would be questioning why I didn't knock on her door since I was so close to her house! My anxiety told me I'd be bothering her, and she would come when she was ready. She would always turn up eventually, but I spent so many hours waiting for people back then I lost count. Funnily enough, we're still in touch now. She's one of those friends where we catch up once in a blue moon and reminisce about years gone by.

The mental struggles continued. 2009 was so lonely, and I'd been on medication that had inadvertently exacerbated my (undiagnosed) anxiety disorder. That summer, I was too anxious to leave the house in case I was attacked. I'd previously walked up the road one afternoon and someone had driven past, and a lad had yelled "MUNTER" out of the window. It shook me up for quite a while. It also added to the little to no self-confidence I had!

When Dr G and I got engaged in summer 2010, I still felt pretty alone, but for my wedding, I picked two female friends. One was Emily, and the other was my university friend, Clare, who had stuck by me throughout my undergraduate degree. I literally couldn't think of anyone else. The rest were either flaky, unreliable friends or I was scared of them.

My hen party was a bit sad too. I arranged it myself because I assumed the bridesmaids were too busy to sort it for me. I invited quite a few people, but in the end, only six people were able to make it: me, the mothers, the sister-in-law, and the two bridesmaids. Yes, it was nice and intimate, but I also felt that I was missing out, as everyone around me had fancy parties with loads of friends, which I never seemed to be invited to.

My bridesmaids didn't let me down, though. They helped me plan my wedding and went shopping with me when I needed them. They turned up and did a great job on the day too. We had such a good time at my wedding weekend that people said they'd love to do it again. Between my bridesmaids, groomsmen and their partners, we had an annual reunion in 2013 and 2015.

In 2013, Clare got married. I was a little disappointed that she hadn't asked me to be a bridesmaid, but I also accepted that my anxiety had stopped me from maintaining the relationship properly after we graduated and I got married. Her hen party was fun, but I was still anxious throughout. I was staying at a stranger's house with a cat that stared at me when I woke up at 5 am after an unsettled night in an unfamiliar bed. It was a group of ladies that were very friendly, but I still felt inferior to everyone. Everyone was more clued up about life than I seemed to be. Everyone was happy to drink, and I didn't have to drive once I was there, so I joined in as best as I could. I was on edge throughout. I don't know if it was because I knew something wasn't right or because of the situation. I went home after that weekend to find out my nana had passed away, and I hadn't had a chance to say goodbye to her.

The wedding itself was lovely. I was reunited with some old university friends that I'd not stayed in touch with. I was slightly less anxious until the evening, where a Ceilidh took place, and neither me nor Dr G were dancers, but we were pressured into joining in, and it was stupidly hot. I tried to join in, but Dr G refused. Everyone was a sweaty mess by the end, but once the dancing finished, we went back to our quiet corner while everyone else mixed and mingled. Despite that, the day was when I was probably the least anxious considering the rest of that year's events.

Meanwhile, in 2013, Emily was having trouble with boyfriends. It later emerged that she'd already split up with the guy she'd taken to my wedding, so the next boyfriend was already on the scene. He came on holiday with us, but halfway through, he had to leave, and then another guy turned up. It was all very strange, and she spent most of the week being emotional and stressed. On the final day, it was Ian's birthday. He was having a meal, and Ed refused to go. Dr G and I went to talk to him, and he confided that if he went, he would have punched Emily's boyfriend, as he was so angry at how he was treating her after he'd witnessed how he'd talked to her earlier in the day. I was too anxious to approach Emily as I didn't know what I was dealing with, but I tried my best to support her. At the end of that holiday, the rest of my friends gave me an ultimatum. "If you invite her next year, we're not coming with you!"

The holiday itself was full of anxiety, and on the first night, we decided to go to the supermarket. Not everyone had arrived yet, but the group decided to go anyway, so I waited in, in case anyone else arrived. I was under the impression they'd fetch the food and come straight back so we could all eat together. That was the year that me and my brother had acquired our first iPhones. We liked winding each other up, and we'd added the Find my Friends app so we could track each other for the laughs. That day they'd been to the supermarket, but they were absolutely ages. I was hungry and getting stressed. I decided to look up my brother's location, and they were pinpointed at a roundabout for quite a while. Immediately, I thought they had been in a crash! But I also told myself to stop being stupid, so I was too scared to message one of them to ask where they were. After what seemed like forever, they came back as if nothing had happened. I was fuming. "Oh, we popped in for a McDonald's," explained Dr G without a care in the world.

2013 was the year I suffered particularly badly with anxiety, but I finally got my diagnosis towards the end of the year. At the height of my anxiety, I was getting worked up about my oldest friend, Tom. He was very unreliable and always forgot my birthday, whereas I always remembered his. I had it in my head that because I didn't attend his wedding, and he couldn't make mine, we had bad blood between us. I wrote him a long Facebook message with the ultimatum that I'd remove him as a friend if he didn't reply. Within twenty-four hours, he replied, explaining that I was still one of his closest friends and he was hurt that I was hurt. That explanation helped me make peace with the situation, and we sorted ourselves out, remaining in contact until the present day.

2015 came by, and the same friends gathered for the annual holiday. Everyone except Emily. I just never invited her. I got tagged in a picture on Facebook and she saw it, sending me a message along the lines of 'I see you're on holiday without me. Thanks.' I was mortified and tried to explain, but she just saw me as weak and spineless. I couldn't argue. I was indeed weak and spineless.

I was literally terrified of people. I couldn't ever say no. I would do anything for anyone who showed me any kind of affection or attention. She blocked me that day. We didn't speak again until I messaged her out of the blue in January 2018 and felt the need to explain myself. I wasn't expecting a reply, but she did, saying she understood, explaining why she was like that but said we'd drifted apart, and she felt we couldn't be friends again. I accepted that. At least I had closure.

COMPLEX FRIENDSHIPS

Dean & Charlie

In 2013, I was just starting with running my gaming community. It wasn't until the September that I had my first official event, but what the community grew into was both astounding and incredibly dangerous at the same time. There was a girl who'd started studying in the department I was taking notes in. Charlie was a bit of an outcast herself, so even though I wasn't a student then, she was a bit older than the average student, so we saw ourselves as having more adult conversation. We'd go for lunch and play badminton together. It was fabulous to finally have what I believed to be an actual best friend!

In the spring of 2014, Dean started attending events. We found out he was pretty lonely, and I remember him asking who the single ladies were in the community after realising I was married. Charlie came up in conversation, as she'd been struggling getting over an ex, so although I swore I'd never matchmake, they were together before I could blink. I remember their first date was our community mini-meet at the local McDonald's. It was love at first sight. It seemed lovely, at least for a while. I was close to both of them. She used to stay the night with us sometimes. She revealed she had severe depression, so I instantly felt like I should look out for her. We were like sisters for a bit, and he was like a brother to me. In the May, she'd stayed over again, but this time I didn't realise about the symptoms of depression, so I let her sleep in until four in the afternoon as I was too scared to wake her. When she woke up, she was disorientated and ended up leaving to catch the train. Then she got paranoid we wouldn't let her back in, so she went into some bushes to go to the toilet and ended up losing her expensive camera. I spent the rest of the evening until it got dark, looking for her camera. I never did find it.

It all started going properly sour around my birthday. They got the train over to my house but missed the stop and ended up in Holyhead. They had to come back, making them about four hours later than planned. I would have done anything for them, though, so I waited patiently, and we still had a good day. Not long after that, I did a Mental Health First Aid course and started to recognise the symptoms, subsequently realising what a mistake I'd made the day she lost her camera. Meanwhile, they'd had a row, except he'd confided in me, and so had she. I advised both of them separately, but he told her what I'd said to him in confidence She ended up snapping and calling me a nosy busybody. Things were just odd after that. She'd often cancel on me, but he'd try his best to turn up.

It was Christmas 2014 when things went really wrong. Dean came to our community event and told me they were moving away. By our New Year's Eve party, we knew it was the last time we'd see him. We promised to keep in touch, and I was emotional, but I tried to understand. They deleted their Facebook account but were still occasionally on Instagram. I followed their every move, no matter how rare. They were married in summer 2018. I was happy for them. Little did I know that lockdown would bring up the 'dirt'.

Dean emerged back in North Wales in summer 2020. I was elated that he was back. We met for lunch with a mutual friend. He told me the whole story since he left that day. She was abusive, and she'd beaten him down. In fact, she'd worn him down completely. The last straw was when she threatened him with a knife. He left that day and said that the police were involved. I just wanted to hug him. It was an emotional day, but it was wonderful to reconnect again. The problem was that so much time had passed, and we'd both changed so much. Our conversations just weren't that natural anymore.

Rob & Dani

This started before the story of Dean & Charlie ended. At a point, we were all in a friendship circle that had been born out of my community. We used to go to each other's houses for games nights and little parties. We grew close, and we did most things together. I took notes in some of Rob's lectures. We chatted a lot, and he was a huge gaming fan and particularly into *Smash* and *Pokémon*. Eventually, he became like a brother to me. I confided in him, and he confided in me. I'd have done anything for him. The parallels were that both Charlie & Rob had severe depression.

I'd completed the mental health first aid course by the time this friendship blossomed. I thought I knew what I was letting myself in for. Yet again, I got in too deep. He got himself into debt, and his mum's house was repossessed. He revealed he had problems at home generally. It was little bits at first. I'd feel sorry for him and lend him money. I even got him a limited-edition Nintendo Console, which he paid me for as soon as he could. At the time, I didn't realise that the amounts he was asking for were gradually getting bigger. I cared so much for him, and I was in the middle of the bad office job too, so I was particularly vulnerable. Later in the term, I ended up half writing his coursework for him because I just wanted him to do well at something in his life.

The last straw was when Rob contacted me whilst I was on holiday, asking me for money. He sounded desperate, so I felt sorry for him and loaned him one hundred pounds. I thought it was weird that he'd asked for it to be transferred into Dani's account rather than his, but I felt sorry for him, so I did it without thinking.

Things started to go sour once the new term had started. Numerous incidents happened, which triggered me every time. They were regulars at our gaming events, but his mood swings were starting to get more erratic. He'd have meltdowns when he lost a game and get angry at his opponents. He once even ended up in a fistfight in the middle of one of our events! We went on a road trip to a Manchester event, and as soon as he lost his game at the tournament, he stormed out into the city centre. We had to go and find him, but I was so anxious about upsetting him further I just waited for him patiently until he had calmed down. His meltdowns got so serious at our local events that we had to ban him for the rest of the year. He turned up to one event, and the room went silent. Later that day, he messaged me to ask me why I was so hostile. I froze in an anxiety panic. My heart had leapt into my mouth. I'd become scared of his volatility.

I always said that my inbox was always open to all my friends, but I started getting late-night messages from Dani saying she was worried about Rob because he'd threatened to kill himself. It was nearly Christmas 2015, it had been one of the hardest years of my life, and Rob wanted to meet up. I no longer trusted him and was terrified of him. I'd just moved house and was so suspicious of him I wouldn't tell him where I lived. When he offered to help me move some boxes, I suggested meeting somewhere neutral instead. He apologised for everything he'd done that day, but I said I could never trust him again, and if he wanted to repair things, he would have a lot of making up to do. I was shaking for every minute of that meeting. I reminded him about the money, and we parted ways.

In August 2016, I sent him a final message about owing the money. It took me a few months to pluck up the courage to send that message, but one hundred pounds was a lot of money to me. I noticed he'd bought tickets to a festival, so he must have some money. I got a very abrupt reply about how I'd be waiting a while. Meanwhile, his now ex-girlfriend Dani had told me he also owed her a lot of money. She was happy to 'pay' that to rid him from her life. I agreed and did the same. The last thing I said to him was fuck off and goodbye! He swore a lot, but I didn't. That sentence was both jarring and satisfying. We never spoke again.

It took me a long while to get over both of those friendships. He broke my heart, and I missed her. I didn't know what to do with myself for months. Fortunately, I had my community guys around me, so at least I wasn't completely alone anymore.

It's Like Tinder for Mums

That's what I was told as a new mum. I was trying to navigate the world of being a new mum, even though mentally I wasn't ready because he arrived three weeks earlier than expected. I was thrown to the edge of depression, but I was discharged from the mental health team while pregnant because I refused the medication. I didn't recognise it at the time, but I struggled to bond with my baby. I learnt very quickly that I didn't cope well with sleep deprivation, so the first two years of my child's life are a fuzzy haze at best.

Although I had my friends from the community, they were mainly younger than me, and my husband, or older, or single, which meant no one was at the same part of life as we were. I went to the local weekly baby group, but I struggled to make friends and would often stay in the same chair and smile politely, making conversation only if I was asked a question. I did get along well with one other older mother, but she went back to work when the babies were a few months old, and my fear of phones and bugging people when they were busy took hold of me, which meant we lost touch within a year.

The NHS gives you so many resources about your baby, I was drowning in leaflets and help books, and I got overwhelmed easily. Amongst these leaflets were recommendations of where you could find friends. One recommendation was the Mush app. Like all my experiences on social media platforms, from the early days of MSN and chat rooms, I was always consistent. I'd be active in whatever community I chose to be part of, and Mush was no different. I didn't tend to ask questions, but I'd answer if I knew what to say. The meeting part was when it didn't quite work out. People would add each other and arrange to meet up. Simple enough, or so you'd think.

The first time I met up with some other mums, it was awkward, but I tried my best to enjoy it. There was a mum with a child of a similar age, and we got along really well. I talked to a few others too, but in the end, I was too scared to ask to swap details, so we parted ways and never met again. The first mum added me on Facebook. It was going fine until she started posting passive-aggressive statuses about other mums who were letting her down because they couldn't meet her every single week. It was a half-hour drive for me. I was a working mum, and weekly just wasn't feasible. I decided to remove her as a friend, as I felt the statuses were aimed at me.

Other experiences from Mush seemed to play out in similar ways. I would always meet a mum once and never see them again. I'd try and arrange to meet up a second time, but they'd always ghost me. I gave up in the end and removed the app as it was making me depressed, and I felt that no one wanted to be our friend. I felt sad for myself and sad for my child.

The second app I tried was Peanut, which had been recommended by another of the leaflets I'd been given. Like Mush, I liked to contribute to discussions, but as this was worldwide, there seemed to be mainly Americans on it. I enjoyed it for a few months, as it gave me people to talk to when I felt that no one In real life cared. This also ended up causing me depression, so I had to remove it. However, not before I'd arranged various meetups, only to be ghosted on the second attempt.

Both of the apps were described as Tinder for mums, which I sighed at. My dating life pre-existed online dating, and Tinder was created after I'd settled down. I was out of my depth, evidently.

Community Cliques

Until lockdown, since about 2014, we had a nice group of friends whose roots were from my gaming community. That group came over to our house for monthly games' nights. We went on road trips together, and we had lots of fun. 2016 was the best year. I turned thirty, the toxic people were gone, and everyone was happy. We went chasing Pokémon for *Pokémon GO*. We spent the end of every party on *Jackbox* laughing about each other and other community members, and it was great fun. We'd go to bed at two or three in the morning, and it felt like a proper party. I worked out over time that the very rare occasion where I didn't get social anxiety or feel the pressure to drink was because I was the host, and it was in my own house.

At peak, there were up to twenty of us, but we started with about six of us. It was nice to feel part of something for once. Most of the group were younger than us. There was one older guy, and one guy was a similar age. The rest of the group were at least four or five years younger. I met quite a few of them through the university as a note taker, and realising we were both musicians and gamers was a great connection to make.

The road trips we went on were awesome. We'd go on day trips to Manchester and Nottingham to see our counterparts and attend their events. I'd get a bit of social anxiety on the trips, but I also knew I was in good company, so I felt safer. We had so many in-jokes and good memories; I didn't want it to end.

I began to struggle when life started changing. People started to grow up. I had a baby in 2017, and everyone said I'd lose my friends. This terrified me. At the same time, I was never going to give up my community, so I tried my best to keep everything going. Once we had the baby, my community events were established enough to run themselves, which helped. We still had tea in the pub after, and it was like old times. The games nights had to drop in frequency, so they turned into quarterly parties, which made them more special to me. Some of the youngest ones dropped off as they moved away or graduated. That was expected, but I was still sad when they left. They said they'd come back to visit, but there was automatically that distance, and in the end, I was still scared of messaging people, so those who were real-life, local friends, became distant virtual friends. We did manage a couple of road trips, but they were very rare after I'd had my baby, as we couldn't justify the childcare with the grandparents. Things ticked along nicely for a couple of years, but I was always anxious.

At the start of 2019, some of the friends were excited, as Hugh Jackman was coming to Manchester, and I overheard them talking about it. I was passionate about the

Greatest Showman and loved Jackman, so I had to be there! We sorted tickets, and we made it. It was beyond anything I could have dreamt of, and I loved it. I even visited my old favourite music shop on Deansgate because we had a snippet of time in the city centre. I was shaky all day, though. Even though it was my home city, it was still a city. There were too many people, and security was tight after a bomb explosion a couple of years previously. I had a bottle of water on me that wasn't technically allowed, but I managed to quietly tell the staff that it was sealed and wasn't a risk. I explained that I needed it to help my anxiety. They accepted that, so apart from being around lots of people, I managed to survive.

I still had the parties back at home in 2019, despite struggling mentally, but I would end up in the other room in the house, with the people playing tabletop games, as I found the room with the big screen too loud. The last games night we had was January 25th, 2020. It was as good a night as any, but I was socially anxious at my own party. I didn't even understand why. I'd laid out white rabbits and red packets because it was Chinese New Year, I was still a good host. The friends were familiar and friendly, so I couldn't understand why I was anxious. The problem with generalised anxiety disorder is that I could be anxious about everything but not be able to identify the trigger. I stayed in that dark, anxious place until May 2020, but the direction changed completely due to lockdown, both for my anxiety and the friendships all around.

Lockdown Lessons

As lockdown got underway in March 2020, we tried our best to keep the community going, but the clique dropped off the face of the earth. Being anxious, I was too scared to check in on anyone or send them a general message, so I assumed they didn't want to know.

When I became a Tropic Ambassador, I found a bit of courage and messaged people to ask them if they were willing to give me a bit of moral support, but most of them said no. I think they saw MLM (multi-level marketing) and put me at arm's length. Some made the excuse that they didn't use products, or they were a soap and water person, but that wasn't what I was asking. It hurt more because they weren't willing to support me as a friend. I took that as they no longer cared about me, so I felt abandoned and lonely. There were very few who supported me at the beginning as far as original friends went. It got to a point where I was scared to message again. As Tropic is a product-based business, I messaged two of my female friends to ask them if I could send them a gift just to let them know I was thinking about them. One of them declined but also explained. It hurt, but I accepted. The other one never replied so I took that as she didn't want to know. That hurt more. I became too scared to message them again. Some of the guys from the clique never really spoke online generally. We only spoke in person, so that didn't change. They just felt extremely far away. A few of those friends popped up for my virtual birthday party but disappeared again. That was mostly confusing, but it was nice, if only for one night.

It got to August, and the community was waning. I was losing my mojo. From the September to December, I distanced myself from my own community events and got involved with the central UK hub more instead after being elected as Head Admin that September. We'd had to ban a member for behaviour on our local server. Dr G and I felt that we didn't have any support from our friends at all. We were mainly on our own. I'd had a breakdown in the early summer. No one had messaged me or checked in at all; I felt like no one wanted to know me.

Meanwhile, I'd constantly been networking online, attending network meetings at least once a month, and building relationships locally and further away. What I came to realise was that I didn't have any friends who were at the same point in life as I was. I had a small child; I ran my own business, both things that the community friends didn't do or have. Networking enabled me to find mums who owned businesses.

It was these people who supported my Tropic venture when it first started. It took some of them a couple of months to get involved, but knowing they were there in the background helped me to keep going. I learnt that you needed to build genuine relationships with people, which took time, but I built up gradually. They were of varied ages. A couple were older, a couple were a similar age, and a couple were slightly younger, but we all had the same thing in common, so we understood each other. There's a particular mindset that you need when you're self-employed, and I didn't find that until September 2020. That was the point I started making real progress. I made so many connections and friendships online throughout the pandemic. I had never felt less lonely than I did then.

Meanwhile, with the community friends, it was the beginning of 2021, and Dr G decided to kick start the community and get online events up and running again. Slowly the friends started making an appearance, but so did my anxiety. I became scared of going online for my own events. Coincidentally I found myself so busy with training and workshops that I'd often be working in the evenings, so I had the perfect excuse to avoid those games nights. It went on like this well into Easter.

It wasn't until late April 2021 that things changed. Two friends, in particular, had triggered me throughout lockdown, and I felt ignored. Mia and Ross were once close friends, but they hadn't spoken to me for over a year. Mia hadn't replied to my gift offer the previous year, so I was too scared to try and message again. There was a national tournament announced, and Ross joined a rival team which upset Dr G, as he was the captain for our team, and at that point, Ross had always been loyal. It was then I finally felt like I had the guts to call them out. I sent them both a Google document. I went back to basics as I did with my relationships. I can't do confrontation, but I can definitely write. I didn't expect either of them to reply, but they did.

I realised by the autumn of 2020, the reason we'd felt ignored for the first lockdown was because everyone else was a key worker, and we weren't. That made me feel guilty for thinking negatively about everyone, and I managed to reconcile in my head, except for Mia and Ross. I think it was simply because once they were so close, and now they weren't, and my brain couldn't work out why, which made me anxious.

Ross replied to say it was my fault, not his, and that I hadn't checked in on him. We'd drifted apart, and I accepted that. I could have been a better friend, but I also felt the need to write back and explain why I'd been that way. Anxiety is never an excuse, but it explains many things. He never replied, but I have to assume that he read it.

Mia replied to say she didn't understand where all the negativities had come from but took the time to reply and explain her point of view. From her side, it was completely innocent, and I immediately felt guilty about all the paranoia I'd had for so long. However, I was also grateful she was willing to explain. I wrote a long document back and explained myself completely. I explained that I was trying to deconstruct my anxiety disorder, and part of the process was this. I explained why I'd thought the things in the first place. In conclusion, we worked out that my anxiety had hampered my ability to cope with the evolving of friendships.

A different friend had recently shared a meme about low maintenance friends. He and I were exactly that. However, my brain wouldn't accept the fact of these particular types of friendships. Going from being 'so close' to 'so distant' just didn't compute. I realised very early on that I wasn't very good at long-distance relationships when it came to boyfriends after trying it with Jonesy, so maybe I'd never really worked that one out.

May 2021 was the month I overcame that. I learnt what the different types of friendships were. I worked on losing my fear of reaching out to people and my resilience. As a result, I feel like I can be a better friend.

BECOMING THE GAMER

When I was little, my dad was into PC games and console games. He had a Dragon 32 on which I remember playing *Frogger*, and I also experienced the original *Pong* and loved it! On the PC, I remember he used to play *Monkey Island* and various pinball games. He also loved *Civilization* and *Up Periscope.*

I don't know how old I was, but my first proper experience of being a gamer was on Windows 3:1 and a text-based *Alice in Wonderland* game. *The Miracle Piano* was my other favourite piece of software. I received a Commodore 64 and a *Zelda* game and watch for my seventh birthday. I was really excited that year. My favourite games on the C64 were *Postman Pat* and *Popeye*, but they took forever to load, so I used to put on *Terminator II* because it was quicker, even though I didn't understand what was going on. I also loved the *Fun School* series.

Between playing on my computer, I remember the *Legend of Kyrandia* on PC being a favourite. I loved following

Brendan on his adventure. I think I played it a bit too much, though, as one night I had a very vivid nightmare that the bad guy, a jester from the game, turned up at my house and took my family hostage while I had to work out how to get out alive. I never found out what happened because I woke up before he killed me! I don't think I dared play the game again after that.

When I was about eleven, I received a classic Gameboy for Christmas. I loved playing *Tetris, Pacman, Mario* and all sorts of games on that, but I would get frustrated when I lost, and that's why my Gameboy had bite marks around it. I knew better than to throw the thing, as I didn't intend to actually break it. A couple of years later, the Nintendo 64 arrived on the scene. It was a couple of years later than everyone else, but we were fairly oblivious to what was going on in the outside world. I loved *Mario 64* and *Zelda: Ocarina of Time* initially, but when I talked to people at school, they all talked about *Mario Kart.* I have to assume my parents couldn't afford all the games, so we borrowed that particular game from a grown-up neighbour who no longer played.

The other game I loved was *Goldeneye.* I got frustrated with that, so I asked a friend to unlock all the fun bits for me. My brother and I just wanted to enjoy paintball mode mostly. When it was just me and him, it was always Oddjob versus Boris, the painter and decorator. We had such a laugh. My favourite game was the *Beetle Adventure Race* game, but no one had heard of that, so I only really played that between me and my brother.

Mario Kart was a different story. Being early teens, everyone was big on *Mario Kart.* People used to invite friends around to play it, and it was great fun. I did get invited initially, and two lads used to invite themselves over to my house to play. I later realised they were probably using me because they didn't have their own console at home. It wasn't a bad way to be, but I never made any lasting friends from that, even though my love for *Mario Kart* never left me.

I was always on and off the PC too. When my dad wasn't using it, we were allowed to play games on it. I particularly loved virtual pinball, *Minesweeper*, the *Lion King* and *Aladdin* games. We evolved over time and played things like *Civilization (1&2)*, *Rollercoaster Tycoon*, *SimCity*, and *The Sims*. He'd allow me to use the internet for a specific amount of time too. What he didn't know was I found his password lying around one morning and wrote it down. I don't know if he knew I'd sneaked on it to email my boyfriend or assumed my mum was using it, but nothing was ever said.

I'd eventually get bullied for liking video games, so I'd hide it. I hid that I collected Pokémon cards by pretending I was minding them for Henry, and by the time I was fifteen, I didn't play video games that much anymore. I just didn't want to get bullied even more than I already was. I wanted to fit in, and a girl playing video games was social suicide.

One thing I did keep up with was PC gaming. I got my own computer in my room when I was sixteen. Jonesy helped me build one using scraps from his local council dump, and it was awesome. I played lots of *The Sims* on there, but it didn't have the internet. I developed a hobby where I liked building computers, so I'd upgrade certain components when I was able to. Just before I was eighteen, I built a PC tower from scratch with Jonesy's help, and I treasured that through university. I was particularly fond of it because it was illuminated. Jonesy was a bit of a pyro geek, and I loved the special effects he was able to create.

I didn't play many video games in my first year at university. I had my PC, but I mainly used it to watch DVDs. I had to go to the university computer rooms if I wanted to use the internet. When I did venture over there, I'd mainly be on MSN or a website for *Diddl* fans. Yet, I nearly drowned in a game called *Runescape* that I sunk fourteen hours a day into for half of my second year of university. The split from Jonesy in the first semester of second year was to blame. I took it hard; the split broke my heart completely, and I was suicidal at one point. There were a couple of school friends on MSN, though, and one of them was playing a game and suggested I join him, which I did, but he had his own friends to play with, so I got chatting to random people. Some were kids who tried to chat up anything that might be female, others were older boys looking for girlfriends, but between all that, there were some decent guys who just wanted to chat. It was rare I came across another female gamer.

Eventually, I made my own clan, and at its peak, it had eighty members, mainly American. It messed up my sleeping pattern, but finally, I started to feel part of something. They cheered me up when I was low, and even the propositions cheered me up sometimes. I remember having a virtual Valentine's date with a lad who said he was nineteen, like me at the time. He served me lobster and chocolate cake, and we chilled out together in the game. The relationship didn't go anywhere because I was always wary of the virtual world and who could be hiding behind things. I never put myself at any risk because I knew better than that, but I made some lasting friends from that part of my life. Most of the kids were struggling with depression or anxiety. Quite a few were on the autistic spectrum, but they loved being in my clan and felt like it was a safe space where they could have fun.

I only stopped playing because the company made an update where they put your cash outside your bank, and that meant it was less secure. Inevitably, I was hacked, and the money disappeared; I was devastated. I'd put thousands of hours into that game, but I lost interest after I was hacked. I also got distracted, as that's when Dr G came on to the scene.

I was depressed, I hadn't eaten properly for months, so in the final semester of my final year in undergraduate university, I bought a PS2 with a dance mat and started exercising every night I was able to. Over the summer months, I played my PS2 and reclaimed my N64 from my parents' house. From there, I rekindled my love for *Mario Kart*. By the time I met Dr G that September, I finally had someone to play it with. Dr G had a SNES, so I went to his place to play sometimes too.

We started dating, and we shared a Nintendo DS in the first few months. Our first joint Christmas present to each other was the Nintendo Wii. We spent hours playing *Mario Kart* on that. We achieved the top rating, the lowest rating, then used homebrew to wind up the hackers because they'd annoyed everyone else. It was great fun, but my eyes started to go really dry as I'd been forgetting to blink. There were plenty of other games we enjoyed too, and the *Mario Galaxy* series was a favourite, also *de Blob* and other *Mario* platformers. I played *Wii Fit* and *EA Active* for a bit and generally felt better about myself. However, none of that helped with my actual anxiety, and eventually, I found myself too busy to keep it up, as I took almost full-time hours with my zero-hours contract.

We were using the Wii and DS until our wedding in 2012. It was only the wedding day when we received a Nintendo 3DS each. It was a complete accident that Dr G and I ended up with two 3DS'. My brother forgot to tick it off the wedding gift list, but that ended up being a great silver lining, as anyone who's had a 3DS knows that *StreetPass* is not something you would want to share on the same console. We didn't realise it at the time, but those 3DS' changed the rest of our lives forever.

SPIRITUALITY & RELIGION

I was brought up in The Church of England. I knew that I was Christian, but I didn't understand the whole Anglican or Catholic thing. I had to assume I was Anglican based on what I learnt over time. As children, my brother and I had to attend Sunday School. My mum was an avid churchgoer, but my dad never went. He would attend the school concerts in the church, as my primary school was attached to it, and the Crib Concert, which happened annually on Christmas Eve. I was christened at the age of four when my brother was a baby.

I also have earlier memories of helping with the Harvest Festival and making hampers for the homeless, building a tower of pennies up a model of the church, and even having a go at bellringing at one point. The children of the church made Christingles once a year and had to sit in the pews holding a lit candle in an orange. Sunday School was fun when I was much younger. We would hear stories from the Bible, make arts and crafts, and colour in story sheets.

There were numerous memorable characters during my time in the church. The organist was an older lady who, in my teens, didn't trust me to play the organ. I was an established pianist by my mid-teens, but she was very protective over her organ.

One of the alto singers was also the chief dinner lady who ran the school kitchen. She was a lovely character unless you got on the wrong side of her. She was terrifying when she was angry! There was also a lovely old man who sang tenor who had a warm heart, but he always confused me with his jokes, but it was him who made me understand sarcasm.

I had a favourite elderly couple who were in the congregation. The guy was a joker, and I remember at the church Christmas Fayre one year, he told me if I stood in the middle of the hall with my eyes closed holding a carrot out, Rudolph the Reindeer and Santa would come and visit me right there. I believed every word he said at the time.

Generally, I was wary of the vicars, as they were seen through my eyes as the 'big' and 'important' people. The curates were usually younger than the vicars, as they were often training to be vicars in their own right. They were always more fun and were tasked with keeping the younger audience engaged with the church community.

The first vicar I remember had a daughter the same age as me, and we used to play at each other's houses until they moved away. The next vicar didn't have any children, and the one after him was a woman who I didn't talk to much. However, the curates were friendly and fun! They always lived in a house just around the corner from ours, and I remember in my early teens, we'd go around in the evening to learn about the Bible, ready for my confirmation that I had in my mid-teens. My proud grandparents attended, and there's a picture of me standing between them with my daft fringe and goofy smile. I don't remember being anxious then.

I think I was around twelve or thirteen when the curate at the time started a youth club for the church's teens. Sunday School was too young for us at that point, but youth club suited us. It was great fun. We'd chat about the Bible, debate current issues, and play with the curate's dog. A couple of the guys I got to know were the ones who popped around for N64 games back in the day. Rounds of *Mario Kart* being the most favourite. The girls were a different story, though. In year six at school, I was friends with identical twins, and I always looked up to them. They were both gorgeous with blonde hair. The confident twin showed off a lot, while the other was shy. The second had a prosthetic arm, so everyone looked after her. These two were part of the youth club.

I was thirteen when the youth club decided to do a weekend away. I was really excited about it, and they let me bring my boyfriend Henry too. It was a weekend full of adventure and activity, including treasure hunts, indoor climbing, sleepovers and plenty of games. However, the first day I arrived, the trouble started. The twins were there, but for some reason, they decided to ignore me. A couple of other friends were also there. I was talking to the other friends, and they told me that the twins had been saying things about me at the session the week before. I became emotional then calmed down before re-entering the building, but I became emotional again when the twins started calling me names. The name-calling concluded with them telling me to sleep on the floor. It was a shared dormitory, and there was a spare bed at the time. One of the staff came in and asked what was up. I cried, and she told me that I could sleep in her room instead, so that's how it was for the rest of the weekend.

Henry looked after me after that, and we managed to enjoy the rest of the weekend. After that weekend, I never spoke to those twins again. On the last day of the weekend, one of the other friends taught me how to climb a tree, then ran off, and I got stuck—awkward! Overall, I had a great weekend and put in my diary that I hoped we could do it again one day. A few years later, I bumped into the confident twin at Youth Orchestra, but she acted as if nothing had happened. I was too anxious to ever talk to her properly.

I occasionally went to Henry's church, and his mum played the organ there, so once I was allowed to have a go on it. That was a precious memory, but I also remember being anxious about the prospect of anyone hearing me play. I started going to a Christian Festival in the late summer when I was fourteen. I was with Henry, and there were three of us in that circle. His best friend, Brian, was also coming with us that weekend. Not before a load of drama happened, though!

Over the earlier summer holidays, there had been a bit of a back and forth over the emails. Brian was more of an evangelist Christian and loved to preach to anyone who would listen. I was curious at the time, so lapped up everything he said, but I got in a bit too deep. He had me promising all sorts of things. The most notable was that he'd only come to the festival with me and Henry if I promised not to do any 'mushy' things: no kissing, no hugging, no couple-type things. I'd been dating Henry for a year by then, and we were pretty into each other. However, to keep the peace, I promised Brian we wouldn't get up to anything.

Come the time of the festival, we went to various talks that we were interested in. We attended the Sunday morning communion, and we got involved in whatever we could. However, there were always quieter times, like early evening after tea or the morning after breakfast. Brian caught us hugging on one occasion. He stormed off and told the curate what we'd done. The curate had a word with us, and the issue was blown up so much it felt like we'd had full-blown sex in front of Brian! It was humiliating and mortifying, and most of all, just a hug. Brian went off on his own for the rest of the day, and I had to apologise to him for betraying his trust. The whole thing felt ridiculous, but I just wanted a quiet life.

I attended the Christian Festival every summer until 2005. It was a great few years. Every year I'd get social anxiety, but by the end, I'd find people to talk to, and it was a space I could always take my boyfriend. Henry came with me, and then later Jonesy attended. In the later years, I became an anxious steward instead. I always asked to be paired with Jonesy so he could look after me, and the latter years of attending the festivals wasn't for the Christian element, it was to get away from the parents so we could have a bit of time alone as a couple.

As the years progressed, my friendship with Brian got frostier, and we started year ten at school not speaking because he'd criticised the way I dressed. "You wouldn't wear your tie that short to a job interview!" he exclaimed on the first day of term. I retorted, "I wouldn't wear a tie to a job interview, you div!" Cue Brian and I not speaking for most of the school year. We did make it up eventually, though, and by the time I was dating Jonesy, it turned out that Brian and Jonesy attended the same church.

This was when things started going wrong. I was really into Christianity then. I studied, read the Bible, and attended the youth club until the curate moved away and the club shut down. I started attending Jonesy's church semi-regularly. He went every week and helped with the sound technology in the church. His church was definitely more high-tech than mine. My church just about had a decent microphone, but his had a large projector and screen, with fancy lighting and various spotlights.

They used to have guest speakers come to do talks at their church. The last one I attended scared me. He was one of those evangelical American self-proclaimed preachers. He was inspiring at the start, but by the end, he was patronising and almost seemed aggressive. It was customary to donate things to your local church, but this guy suggested that if you didn't donate, you'd go to hell! As a teen with no money, I couldn't afford to donate, so that made me on edge. Surely, I wouldn't go to hell just because I couldn't afford to donate to the church?

Around the same time, my church had problems. My mum was being bullied, and I didn't realise until she ran out of the church in tears. There was a big bully of a woman who used to run the tea and coffee at the back of the church. I don't know what happened, but a switch went off in my head. If that's how they treat my mum, I don't want anything to do with this place anymore. We never went to church again. My mum still considers herself Christian, but I have considered myself agnostic ever since.

At university, I avoided religion completely—I'd had enough. I definitely wasn't Atheist, but I wasn't sure what to believe anymore. Occasionally one of my housemates in third year would invite me to her church, but the thought sent shivers down my spine, so I never dared to try again.

However, I was a note taker for several years in the local university, and one of the opportunities I got was to take notes for a theology student. This opened up all sorts of interesting discussions, which I listened to intently. I learnt about Islam, Sikhism, Judaism and Christianity. I also took notes in the Psychology of Religion module. The summary of all that was, I learnt to appreciate multiple religions and how they worked. I also noticed that they all basically followed the same fundamental principles, which is to be nice and don't do bad things. Of course, expanding on that, there are varying rules depending on what bit of faith you followed because even within the main headings, there are sub-religions. The conclusion I drew from all that learning was that people basically have faith to have a purpose.

I had a secular wedding, despite a query from a person at my old church asking if I was going to return to my hometown to get married. I wanted a Welsh wedding, so we chose a castle in North East Wales, booked the registrar and planned our secular readings. The only requirement was from the in-laws: Dr G's family had always had 'Calon Lân' at their weddings, so I had to fit it in somewhere. I put it during the wedding breakfast just before the cutting of the cake. It fitted nicely; it just didn't go to plan either!

There was the question of a religious blessing happening after the wedding day itself, but it never happened. I know my grandparents being religious themselves, would have loved that. However, they'd just been diagnosed with cancer and dementia, respectively, so we chose not to plan anything else, as they couldn't attend my wedding in the first place. I never returned to my old church either. I didn't give religion or spirituality a second thought for several years. I chose not to christen my child when he was born and never gave it a second thought.

Fast forward to 2020 and lockdown. On my journey of self-development, the question of spirituality came up. I read *The Universe Has Your Back* by Gabby Bernstein after a recommendation from the Vision Board Queen, which changed my whole perspective. It talked about the Universe, but by the end, it referred to the Holy Trinity or a similar notion, which was familiar to what I learnt growing up, but this wasn't Christianity. It was looking towards the concept of the Law of Attraction. I looked into this law and adopted some of its principles. I also became the pianist I was always meant to be and started playing more publicly from Christmas 2020.

At the start of 2021, I met a guy from the local community. He'd set up a monthly meeting for the community. I didn't realise he was religious at first, but he followed The Baha'i Faith, which I had never heard of before. I'm completely certain that I don't wish to follow a religion ever again, but it's always interesting to listen to other people's stories and perspectives. Every month, each member contributed a reading, poem or music, and I would usually write them a poem. It was great to get out of my comfort zone as I was used to only writing love poems to my boyfriends or husband over the years, but I've written about different topics now. In one meeting, he commented that I have a sense of spirituality about me. I'd never thought about it, but how do I see spirituality? I see spirituality as having faith in what you're doing—having a purpose, having principles and being true to yourself. Yes, I am spiritual!

STREETPASS CHANGED OUR LIVES

We arrived home from our wedding with our new *3DS*s and wished we had local friends to play games with. A month or so later, Dr G saw an advert for a competition with *Mario Kart 7*. It was to race against people in your region, and the top two won a ticket to an exclusive event in Birmingham. I didn't think I'd win, but when it was the Females in Wales round, only three of us entered. We worked out that the more time we spent on it, the more points we'd get, so two of us raced together. The other person cheated and got a random nameless person to race with her and therefore came first because she always went on at times she knew we wouldn't be on. However, I got the second ticket, as the third lady (who came second) decided she didn't want to go to Birmingham after all and let me have the ticket instead.

I was excited and terrified at the same time. The realisation that I had to go to a city. A CITY! I had to stay in a hotel and get a train. The whole concept filled me with dread, but I also knew I had to be there. I was so anxious about the day, but this also worked to my advantage. All contact was through Facebook, so I suggested anyone attending joined a group so we could connect before the day. Not everyone joined, of course, but a handful did, and that handful are still friends to this day. It also made the day a lot easier for my anxiety. I felt like I already knew some people, so I wasn't half as terrified as I might have been.

Dr G and I travelled down on the train the day before and met Ian for pizza as he lived that way. It was lovely, and they'd just introduced gluten-free options to the restaurant too, so I didn't have to miss out. The nightlife was vibrant, but it was also my worst nightmare, so we went straight back to the hotel room as it felt much safer.

On the day of the event, I didn't want it to end. It was phenomenal, and everyone who'd joined the group was there. We had an established group of friends to hang out with. I wasn't anxious apart from when the competition started. While I was on stage, my heart was pounding, but chemically, my brain couldn't distinguish between excitement and nerves—I could feel both.

I ended up coming third overall. I won a mini-shell trophy. The second and first place females were part of my group, so we all congratulated each other like old friends. The prize was also a year's supply of 3DS games. I got a little bit too excited at that point. The Nintendo production team had heard we'd had a Mario-style wedding and wanted to know more. I was interviewed for Nintendo TV, but it was edited out. When they asked me what I'd advise young gamers, I got verbal diarrhoea and went on a rant about how sexist the adverts had been recently with all the horrible pinkness—epic fail. That was my moment of fame gone like that. For the final edit, there was just a two-second clip of me speaking into a microphone with no sound.

Coming home from the event, we were buzzing, but again we had no one local to play our Nintendo games with. A month later, I created a Facebook group. I quickly realised I had no idea how to meet people and tell them about us. I was too scared to start conversations, especially with strangers. The first year, I used to StreetPass with random people and have my group name in my message. A couple of people found the group, but most didn't look. When I went to yoga in the local chaplaincy, I used to get StreetPasses, so I eventually found out who they were, and they invited me to a couple of *Mario Kart* sessions, but nothing ever came of it, as I was too scared to follow up. There was also a lecture I took notes in where they used to play *Mario Kart* in the break. After several weeks I finally plucked up the courage to ask them if I could join in. I only managed one session with them, and then the term ended, and everyone moved on.

We found a guy on Twitter running a little virtual community in Llandudno, so we teamed up with him and created our regional group instead. StreetPass North Wales was born, and it wasn't long after that we found Manchester had an equivalent group. Dr G, my brother and I went on a day trip to their *Big Luigi* event, and although I was very anxious, they made us feel at home. By the end of the day, we'd met the hosts, and they promised to put us in touch with the main support. A few days later, we were part of a UK hub. There were groups scattered across the country. It was amazing to know others were out there, and I was so excited for what it could become. The hub supported us to get our first event set up, and we officially started in September 2013. It was an incredibly rocky start, but the main priority initially was collecting those puzzle pieces from StreetPasses.

A FIVE-YEAR VENDETTA

After our first event with StreetPass North Wales, in a pub with loud sweary football fans, we had to find a new venue. I looked around town, but everything was too expensive. We were a not-for-profit, voluntary-run community, so it had to be a free venue. I was getting very anxious, as it took a lot of guts to speak to people at various venues. However, I did it because I was determined to make it work. We'd also made links with the university's gaming league, and they'd attended our first event. I'd asked the president for help with finding a venue, but he wasn't very helpful. Dr G suggested trying the university. I found the cinema room could be booked through the café in the centre of town, so before every event, I would go in person to the café to book it. Initially, the gaming league got their backs up because someone had told them we'd nicked their name to book our events. I'd booked it under my own name and also said we were a gaming group, but apparently, the people in charge put two and two together and got seven. The next thing I knew, Keith from the gaming league was trying to shut us down.

When I heard what had happened, I tried to correct the booking and make it clear that we were separate from the gaming league. We emphasised that we were a community with a mix of students and the public. Most times I made the booking, I saw it written down in their diary, yet when I turned up on the day of the event, the security team would usually have no record of the booking. A few times, I would end up in tears on the phone asking what I was supposed to do as I'd seen them write it in the diary. This went on until 2017. Three years of hell every time we attempted to book the venue. We had a bit of let-up in the summer months because we booked a venue in a different part of the university. We liked the summer treat of a venue that also sold food. Due to it being manned, there was no issue about it being locked, except when the message didn't get through there either. Safe to say, venue securing was incredibly stressful and anxiety-inducing.

Keith's attempts to sabotage us were unsuccessful. However, he was still seething, as when he got elected to a sabbatical position on the students' union, he came into a place where one of my friends worked and started gloating that the first thing he was going to do was block me from using venues. He didn't realise that both Dr G and I were members of staff, so we could book venues for free whenever we needed to. I plucked up the courage to arrange a meeting with him when he was elected and offered an olive branch. In that meeting, I told him that I was a member of staff, and we were happy to work with him. It was one of the most awkward meetings I'd ever attended, and at the last minute, I had to ask a friend to sit with me for moral support. I was shaking through the whole thing, but we survived, and we came out feeling triumphant. I left him with the parting words, "I'm here until I die. What about you?" The vendetta lasted until he left the university, having attended for five years.

It was 2018 when I next bumped into him. I was playing the piano at a local wedding fayre, and he was looking around with his fiancée, having been recently engaged. I was feeling slightly more confident that day, and as soon as I spotted him, I said cheerily, "Hi, how are you?" Then I went on to say, "I can adapt gaming music for your wedding as well as the traditional favourites." I finished my statement with a massive beam. I watched him visibly squirm and make his excuses for the toilet. His parents smiled politely, and his fiancée politely said thank you, then awkwardly shuffled away. In my head, that was my revenge, and it felt good, especially that I think he knew he'd lost after all those years.

I think it was the same year that the current president of the gaming league attended one of our events and apologised on behalf of the whole of the gaming league for the bad feelings going back and forth over the years. I accepted. We didn't have any bad feelings towards them apart from not understanding where on earth all the hate had come from.

CHWIFIO'R FANER AR GYFER GOGLEDD CYMRU

'Waving the flag for North Wales' has been the motto (in Welsh) on my profile page for the UK hub for as long as it has existed. Aside from a five-year vendetta, and multiple problems with venue bookings, we have soldiered on. It was my first passion, and I'd lost interest in being a musician for a couple of years and thought I was meant to be in the office workers' world. However, running this community with all its ups and downs helped me cope with the nightmare job, as I had somewhere to channel my creative energy into.

I later learnt that the root of my anxiety disorder was an extreme fear of being judged. Due to that, when I started my local community, I created a second Facebook profile and blocked all my original friends who I thought would mock me for being a gamer. I hid from them completely. It confused my gaming friends slightly, though, as they were friends with 'both' of me and never knew which profile to tag. I kept this up for quite a few years. I was afraid to show my face. I didn't like photos unless they were group ones, and I didn't like adding strangers to my main profile. I kept my two online lives separate until I created my brand, The Tropic Pianist Gamer.

At our first event in September 2013, a couple of guys offered to take some *Mii* hats around town and got some attention for our event. The university gaming league people attended and joined in, but in the end, our co-host won the trophy, and one of them kicked up a fuss, so I ended up getting anxious and handing the trophy to second place (gaming league president) and apologising. The vendetta began not long after that event too.

The second event was in the local Caffè Nero. It was awkward and anxiety-inducing. They'd not reserved the table as I'd requested, so we had to squash into a corner, and only two of us stuck around for the whole thing. In November, we held two *Pokémon* events. We planned the first one and found ourselves ahead of everyone else from the hub, so when the Nintendo guy asked everyone if they'd put on a *Pokémon* event, we'd just missed the window. However, he said we could do a second one. I got flustered because these events were bigger and featured semi-professional players paying us a visit. The event took place earlier in the month, and we had prizes supplied to us, but I got a bit overwhelmed easily. I carefully planned out which prizes to give away for competitions and which ones to give for the raffle. However, the event didn't work out that way. The *Pokémon* tournament was so quick it ended and left a massive gap in the schedule, so a co-host suggested running a second tournament, just for fun. My brain, for some reason, went into panic mode, and agreed, then gave all the raffle prizes away to the winners of the second tournament. We just about managed to scrape enough raffle prizes together, but I was mortified.

The second *Pokémon* event was a national qualifier, which meant the winners had the opportunity to go to London for the final. Dr G and I attended the London final too, and that was our first chance to meet other founders from the hub. It was an awe-inspiring but terrifying day. In early 2014, we had an event where only four of us were present. My anxiety started telling me we'd failed, but we pushed on, and the game we featured was a four-player game anyway, so that mini-meet worked out fine.

It was then I got the first bit of office job, though. I was a proper member of staff at the university. That's when I realised that I could book the venues as staff, so from then on, I just booked it under my name instead. We used the cinema room most of the time and the bar in the student halls campus in the summer. In between big events, we would have mini-meets in the evenings at a local pub. This pub had a nice alcove that we could hide away in, and we used to love playing *Mario Kart, Luigi's Mansion 2, Tetris* and other things. At peak, thirty people turned up to our mini-meet, and we ended up staying late and playing *Cards Against Humanity*—it was spectacular!

My first ambitious plan was to host a national event for all the StreetPass groups. Summer Holiday in North Wales was born, and some of the other founders pledged to come over. None of the members seemed to be that up for it, though, and in the end, we couldn't arrange complimentary transport or accommodation, so I was a bit naïve to assume it could work. However, we pushed on, and the lady who ran the Basildon community visualised *Tomodachi Life* crossed with Eurovision—Miivision! We laid it out like Eurovision, and I booked the local student bar as a venue so that people could have food. One of the Nottingham members baked some special cakes. It was all planned out. I was anxious throughout and rounding the various groups up to take part and then collecting the votes caused so much stress. When one of the London communities tried to sabotage the voting, I was majorly triggered and went into panic mode. Thankfully, in the end, everything worked out. We had founders from seven different parts of the UK coming to take part and a good handful of song entries to vote on. The day itself was exciting, and it was our first chance to get to know some of the others on our home turf too, so going for a drink after the event, I felt fairly calm compared to usual.

Over time we forged some proper friendships from the community. We used to go to the pub after an event to chill out and review how we thought the event went. It was just what I needed after a hard week at the office. The Pokémon Society also emerged around this time, and I think everyone was as anxious as each other having our first meeting. It was a little bit awkward, but we also knew we wanted to work together, so we had collaborations every year until it ceased to exist again a few years later.

In late 2014, the communities were going crazy for the newly released *amiibo*, and I ended up with a library that friends could use when they came to visit. I would often take a selection to events for people to use too. If you missed the pre-order, you missed out, so if I was out or in a lecture, I'd be there on my phone out of sight, with the page open, ready to press that click to buy button.

The Christmas event in 2014 was incredible. The friends got us a card to say thank you for running an awesome community and had all signed it. I got a bit emotional about that, and I was so touched. At this Christmas event, we had the opportunity to do a qualifier for *Smash* and then head to Birmingham to the finals at the end of January, where we met up with other founders and communities. It was an inspirational weekend, but I was so determined to be useful that I sat on the reception desk all day. That meant I didn't get hit by social anxiety, but I also didn't get a chance to chat properly with anyone except my reception buddy.

Rob & Dani were around at this point and were very involved with the community. At multiple points, I'd get too involved with Rob because I wanted him to be ok, and he was wavering on drowning with his depression. He also had an anger problem, so after a bit of a fistfight at a summer event, throwing a controller at the wall and generally displaying disrespectful behaviour to others, which worsened over time, we decided to ban him for the rest of the year. That triggered my anxiety majorly. I cared so much about Rob, and I felt responsible for him sometimes. I just wanted him to be ok, but I didn't realise he was dragging me down with him. The community still survived, and the other friends we'd made stuck around and supported us.

The biggest event I'd ever co-hosted, North vs South, happened in 2015. It happened to be on the day of my birthday. It was the most stunning day, but it was also at the end of the most stressful week in my office job. One of the other organisers had stressed me out so much I'd had a breakdown the day before my Welsh exam—I was a wreck. On the day of the event, one of the North Wales members had a meltdown. Rob had a go at me, telling me he'd put on a front all day, but he'd hated every moment of it. I was so determined to make the event the best day ever I was devastated. To top that off, I also forgot to clear my StreetPasses, so not only did I not get everyone's 'hit', but barely anyone knew it was my birthday. I was also gutted when some of the group staying over chose not to join my birthday meal. Although my logical brain understood, my emotional brain felt unwanted. Nevertheless, the ones that weren't local stuck around. We had a lovely meal and witnessed one of the best sunsets I've ever seen. Those friends reminded me to look back on the positives rather than the negatives.

In September 2015, Joe (the Nintendo community guy) married his best friend, and we were lucky to be invited to the evening party, but we'd planned an event for the same day, which we left in the hands of two regulars. Only two additional people turned up, as we'd popped in to set up with them. I was devastated. I remember crying in the doorway and saying we'd failed. Dr G reassured me, but I was so ashamed about that meeting that it never appeared in the official blog, and it rarely, if ever, gets mentioned when reminiscing.

2016 was the year of the *Pokémon Go* craze. That was a great help for social anxiety. I had a little bit more confidence, and when the game came out, I led a few walks around the local area for my community and got to know a few other people too. It was a great year for events, there were no major dramas, our close friends were joining us for every post-event party, and we had regular games nights around at our house. I'd say it was the year of parties, and I came across as confident, even though deep down, the anxiety was as high as ever. Professionally, I had just set up as a freelance piano teacher but was too scared to get out there properly. I only had my friend, Hannah, as a guinea pig for a few months, which meant I had plenty of time for gaming and planning events.

2017 was the year I had my baby. The year started with a day trip to London to the exclusive Switch preview in London. Joe arranged for coaches to pick up the various groups. We drove to Warrington, then caught the bus with the Liverpool and Manchester guys. I was anxious all day, but I was looked after too. It was a fab day, and I wanted it to be my mission to meet and say hi to any fellow founders. I got around most of them and even organised the group photos. I had to sit at the front of the bus there and back because travelling that far made me anxious. I liked to be able to see what was going on. There was a bit of an awkward moment when we got dropped off at Warrington on the way back and realised we'd left two of our group on the bus as they'd fallen asleep, and no one had noticed.

I'd planned all my events a year in advance, so I thought I'd put one on the sixth of May. It was three weeks before the baby was due, and I would be fine to host. However, the world doesn't work like that, and my baby was born on the fourth of May. I would have still been in hospital on the sixth if I hadn't discharged myself. I made it to the start of the event and popped in to say hi. I'd delegated all the duties to our regular, reliable members, but I was nervous as it was the first proper event of the community that I'd not been able to host myself. They ran it like clockwork while Dr G and I had to return to the hospital to feed the baby. We made a point of making it back for the group photo at the end, though.

2017 was the year we changed venues too. We realised that a big open plan lecture room was bookable, which was our main venue until lockdown. This coincided with our re-branding too. Joe had sorted out branding for the hub, so the regions followed suit, and we had permission from Nintendo itself to use Nintendo in our names, as long as we made it clear that we were independent communities. Nintendo North Wales emerged.

In June 2017, we paid our counterparts in South Wales a surprise visit. This went slightly wrong, as they didn't like surprises, so they took it as we came to hijack their qualifier when all we wanted to do was see friends and connect. This triggered my anxiety majorly, so by the time we got there, we received nothing but hostility. I was on edge for the rest of the day and couldn't enjoy it. The founder did apologise via message after we'd left the venue. The following month, two of my group got the opportunity to visit Nintendo HQ for the day. Dr G and I had to decline due to having a newborn baby to look after, but it was great to give the opportunity to some of our most established members.

In the September, a group of our *Splatoon* players took part in the northern final, hosted by Newcastle. I'd only just finished expressing milk then, so physically, it was a bit more difficult for me, but we could stay the night in a hotel. It was an awesome weekend, and I saw it as a chance to make connections, although, as usual, social anxiety hit me. I talked to the hosts but was too afraid to introduce myself to anyone else and sat in the corner most of the time I was there.

The rest of 2017 was a complete blur, I was severely sleep-deprived, but the day of the event was always the kid-free day where we could be ourselves again, so we savoured those events and the post-event chill in the pub. We concluded the year with a proper Christmas meal, and it was great fun. The community was flourishing, and people felt like it was their safe space where they could be themselves. By then, we easily had thirty people at our monthly events.

In 2018 we had plenty of popular events. The highlight was in the summer, when we had visitors from far and wide, particularly for the *Splatoon* event, which coincided with a national *Splatoon* tournament I'd been hosting for the UK hub. North Wales had two teams, and they both did pretty well. I was gaining confidence bit by bit, and it was that Christmas that I debuted on the keyboard for the Christmas quiz.

In the November, we had the opportunity to attend the convention MCM in Birmingham, and some of our members were able to meet the developer of *Splatoon*. It was a phenomenal atmosphere, but yet again, social anxiety hit me, so I sat in one place for ages, unable to try and talk to newer people.

2019 was the year when Nintendo North Wales did everything differently. We'd started thinking outside the box more and included things like upside-down racing and blindfolded games. We also tried too hard in the March by having all the games, and I got stressed because I couldn't keep up with what was going on. In April, I got carried away and hosted a massive Yoshi Egg Hunt. It was great fun, but there was always someone who moaned, so I wondered if I'd done it wrong and focussed on what went wrong rather than the fact that most had enjoyed it.

May was the Nintendo *Labo* release. One of my hobbies is paper crafting, so that was right up my street. I made a full-scale obstacle course for the *Labo* bug to run, and everyone loved it. I was feeling confident that day. However, June 2019 was the first year we attended Anglesey Comic Con. We had fun that day, except it was my community members who helped out and got talking to people. Anxiety made me sit at my table most of the day and not move.

The *Splatcon* tournament was in its second season that summer and Nintendo North Wales' first team won it, so that was a proud moment for our community. At the Christmas event, I got my keyboard out again for Quiz Done Differently. I was so shaky and barely managed to play it, but I survived, so I felt triumphant after hearing great feedback from the members. We finished on another high with a group Christmas meal to celebrate.

In January 2020, we did our first ever charity event, playing *Just Dance*. I even joined in the dancing as I'd lost weight and felt a little bit better about myself physically. For some reason, after that event, my anxiety hit me again, but it was full-on, and I couldn't work out how to stop it.

The February event was the final event we had before lockdown. It was based on *Smash* as the hub ran qualifiers for a national final. I don't remember much about that day, except I functioned. I was so anxious I barely moved from my seat. I didn't talk to any of my friends. To make matters worse, they barely spoke to me either, so my anxiety told me I must have done something to upset them. Dr G noticed I was bad, so had a word with Mia in the middle of the day, but she was completely oblivious. I thought maybe my anxiety would sort itself out once we'd been for tea at the pub. Everyone except for three people cancelled. There were usually between ten and fifteen of us, and I was gutted. My anxiety told me everyone hated me. I sunk into depression.

Just before the pandemic hit, Dr G and I were invited to Nintendo HQ. We got to meet the more recent Nintendo Community Manager, Mack. Alas, after that epic weekend, we ended up in lockdown, so all regional plans were cancelled, and we moved completely online.

We moved on to our *Discord* server and tried to honour the event dates we'd already booked. The more events we did, the less I was interested. It was draining, and those who took part did nothing but complain and argue with each other. This included a vendetta! A kid had complained about the *Smash* rules. As a community, we put on fun tournaments for *Smash*, which generally meant the hardcore players didn't like it, but our aim is to be inclusive, not exclusive. I took their ideas on board and said they could write the next ruleset. I was working one evening, and before I knew it, it had all kicked off in a group chat, and the kid had personally attacked Dr G on the chat, then deleted it before I got a chance to read it. We decided to ban them. They felt so wronged that they re-entered the server using a VPN, completely flouting the ban. They ended up getting a lifetime ban. Showing no remorse several months later, they then started attacking various community members in certain multiplayer games and trying to turn our members against us.

I lasted until August, then decided I'd had enough. This queen of consistency was ready to pack it all in, but she'd put her heart and soul into it and wasn't ready to leave either. I shut down all events, and Nintendo North Wales did nothing between August and December 2020 because of that.

What the kid hadn't bargained for was them telling everyone I was a liar when I already had a reputation across the national hub for being the most honest, reliable and trustworthy person in the community. It boggled my mind, but by then, I'd done a lot of self-development, so my resilience was a lot higher. I put faith in my reputation preceding me, and it died down pretty quickly this time.

In January 2021, I saw a new lease of life for our community. Dr G picked up the slack and took charge of online events, bringing regular sessions back again. He understood that I was all about the physical events, so although they had fun, I dipped in and out when I had the energy or time.

It was so good to get the physical events back in July 2021. We started with outdoor meets, and with my new confidence, I rocked up in my *Tetris* crop top and leggings, with my softshell Nintendo North Wales jacket. The best bit was having my community back together like old times. Catching up, everyone was so grateful just to see each other again in real life.

We started back with indoor meets in October 2021. It was such a relief to be back, or at least halfway to normal again. It was different, though. We were lucky that a shop in Llandudno offered us their upstairs space as a temporary solution. Numbers were capped at twelve (then fifteen) and ticketed. Our events have always been, and will always be, free to attend, but we needed to ticket it, so we knew who to expect. People were advised to take lateral flow tests on the morning of the event, as well as wear masks while attending, and this is how it would be for the foreseeable future, but everyone was just glad we were back.

HOLDING THE NATIONAL FORT

I started my regional community in 2012, met the contacts in 2013, and built a relationship with the head of the hub, Joe, over the years. As a region, we were always one of the first to get involved and jumped at the chance of any opportunities thrown our way.

Our very first outing to the more central circuit was to London in December 2013. The Nintendo manager had arranged the final of a regional *Pokémon* tournament to end in London and invited all the relevant group leaders along to support their players. I was terrified, but there was no way I was going to miss this opportunity.

We caught the train down to Euston, which I just about survived, but I point blank refused to catch the tube, so we had mapped out our walk across central London to the venue. We met a few long-distance travellers who'd come from Scotland at the station, so we had people to walk with. The day was incredible, but I was really shaky and shy. A couple really looked out for me that day, and we formed a friendship from that. She was outgoing and bubbly and had every bit of confidence I could only dream of having. He made me feel more at ease too. When the food arrived, the manager had heard I could only eat gluten-free, so cooked a gluten-free pizza. What he hadn't told us was that all the pizzas were gluten-free, so everyone else ate them. I survived the day on leftover wedges.

When the event ended, I was anxious about walking back through London, but there was a group of us, one of whom had a massive standee to carry, so I felt like if anyone drew attention to us, it would be him. I was quiet most of the evening. We ate at Wagamama's, and it was great to connect, but the rush back to the train station was terrifying. The station was so busy, and I was afraid of getting squashed or trampled on. I was so quiet on the way home I didn't want to draw any attention to myself and sat by the window with Dr G protecting me on the aisle side. We survived.

Between 2013 and 2016, we tried to do road trips where we could. The regulars from StreetPass North Wales would visit Manchester and Nottingham mostly, but Dr G and I also made a trip to Banbury to see the couple we'd connected with at the London event in 2013. I helped run the tombola at their event and tried my best to be confident, but I was still very shaky and nervous all day. When I bumped into a couple of familiar faces, I was slightly at ease, but conversations didn't flow naturally either. Awkward silences were so typical for me back then.

At the start of 2015, we went to Birmingham for a national final for *Smash*. I had a grand idea that I wanted to meet as many people as possible that weekend. I definitely did, but I also didn't talk to anyone, as I signed up to help with the registration desk, so most only got a greeting, and then I never spoke to them again. Some of us had stayed over for the weekend, so it was there that Joe quietly told me that he was going to be the next Nintendo community manager, replacing the original one. That weekend was absolutely phenomenal.

By the end of the year, Joe explained that due to a conflict of interest, he needed some admins to help him with the Facebook group. There were a few volunteers, and I was one of them. He chose four, including some of the most established and active group admins. We also had a website and social media, which he left to one guy, Fred.

What ensued in the next five years was very rocky. The other three admins just sat there. One was always too busy with life, one was forgetful, and another stressed about everything and would always question things whether it needed questioning or not. It was impossible to decide anything, and basically, nothing happened for a while. The hub used to provide national qualifiers for groups to participate in, but this was run by Nintendo UK (Joe), so admin played little if any part in that.

There was a bit of drama every now and again over the years. In the early days, Joe mainly dealt with it. We had an issue with someone getting arrested for grooming a teenage girl. Another case was when the police were involved, but the guy in question claimed innocence—it was him vs her. That was the first time I was involved. Thankfully one side had evidence, so it was clear cut how we needed to act, though it was sensitive and had to be kept confidential from the other group leaders. Joe relinquishing hub responsibilities in 2015 meant that anything else that happened was the new admins' responsibility, but Joe still had the final say on who was admitted into the hub.

In 2016, Joe welcomed a guy into the hub. Other founders, including myself, had voiced concern about this person before he was admitted, and every month he was in the hub, he proved us right. His attitude was against everything that the hub stood for. He didn't understand or respect our ethos and was simply in it for the freebies. It took us until early 2017 to remove him after he became offensive to me. Since I was involved, one of the other admins stepped up to deal with it. She was firm, but death threats and general insults were thrown her way for a bit. She sadly had to take it, which affected her mental health for a while. The rest of the time, little drama happened. Things just ticked along like a timebomb.

Despite the admin being mostly inactive, Fred was very active, so he and I eventually worked together instead. It was ok, but at times it was awkward. He was an anxious dyslexic but would never ask for help. As the social media guy, his posts were full of mistakes, and despite being corrected and called out several times, he never seemed to learn or want to fix it.

It wasn't until 2018 and the first *Splatoon* tournament that we started doing our own central tournaments. One of the more active founders proposed that it be run by the hub itself for the first time. The *Splatoon* tournament ended up being a bit of a mess. The guy tried to run it solo and unexpectedly let in a load of teams, so he struggled to cope with the workload. Fred wasn't very helpful, and it was after a few weeks he suggested cancelling the whole thing.

I'd been watching from the sidelines, as I was still sleep-deprived with baby brain, but I'd be damned if this was getting shut down. The tournament organiser was panicking, so after he had an argument with Dr G over rules, I decided to step in and offer a solution. I became an Assistant Tournament Organiser (TO) and worked with him on a solution. I saved the first tournament, and we made it work so well that people asked for it to return the following year. I didn't take the credit for that. I was very much behind the scenes. Sadly, this meant that Fred took most of the praise instead.

However, I realised that, as the hub, we could do more central things to bring the communities together. I know that the new Nintendo Community Manager, Mack, was very enthusiastic about this idea, but I was met with resistance from the other admin. One of them saw the hub solely as somewhere to flag where to find the regional groups, and that was it. One was scared about what it might involve, and one agreed but was also not very forthcoming at replying generally. I, therefore, started making plans with Fred. At least someone was actively interested. I wrote up a plan. We would have two or three major tournaments a year and little side tournaments in between.

Over the next couple of years, we had *Puyo Puyo Tetris* (teaming up with PuyoGB), *Runbow* (official prizes from the developer, 13AM.) *Pokkén, Smash, Mario Kart, Mario Maker* & *Overcooked.* People loved the inter-group tournaments, and although they weren't without their niggles, overall, they were a success. Meanwhile, the other admins still weren't really involved. They just watched from the sidelines. They did complain at one point that things needed to be more transparent, so I agreed that we'd post the rules for each main tournament in the Facebook group for consultation before pressing the green button. It worked well generally.

The second *Splatoon* tournament happened in 2019. It was highly fuelled and great fun, but the lesser able teams felt inferior. There were a lot of 5-0 scores, and by the end of it, they were feeling a bit rubbish. At the knockout stage, one team even gave up because they were fed up with losing all the time. One decision I'd made the previous year was to conduct a survey so that all participants could have their say on how they thought it went and how they would improve it if we did it again. Behind the scenes was a mess. The rules were airtight, but it was just me, the original organiser and Fred. The other two kept falling out with each other. I ended up stuck in the middle a lot of the time. It didn't do my mental health any good, and I nearly suffered from burnout after that. Fred didn't speak to me for most of the tournament, so at times I was running it solo. The rest of 2019 was a low for me, mentally.

I remember the feedback from the survey, as we did a voice chat to summarise it. It ended up being an argument. I flipped at Fred; he flipped at me. We made up with each other, but I took it to the admin, explaining the problem. We agreed to have a voice chat-based meeting to discuss issues, but only one other admin attended. I took notes to relay back to the remaining admin, but it took months between one reply and the next. I eventually gave up and let Fred just do his thing because I was tired of fighting. We had a system, and it worked. It was just far from ideal.

In March 2020, we were invited to Nintendo HQ for a founders meet. I was anxious, but I had to go. I assumed

I'd have to go on my own because of childcare, but thankfully the in-laws offered to take the kid for two nights. Dr G offered to drive us straight there. If I'd have had to get a train, I would've had to go through central London and catch a tube train. This was my worst nightmare. The height of my anxiety was about cities and public transport. The weekend travelling went like a dream, and it was nice and straightforward. We couldn't initially find the car park, but once we'd parked up and found the door to the Travelodge, we were settled for our two-night stay.

The event was extraordinary, but that didn't stop social anxiety from hitting me again. I ended up chatting to familiar people, sticking to my table for the day because I was scared of new people. However, I had to do a little speech about the Covid-19 situation. There's always that one person who asks all the awkward questions, and I could feel myself going red. I was already shaky because of nerves, but he nearly made me cry in front of everyone. Thankfully, someone else noticed and shut him up in time.

The rest of the day went well, the food was great, and I even managed to set up a *Tetris* game with over twenty of us. I was still socially anxious by the end, though, despite the good day. I wanted to go for tea with whoever didn't have to dash off, but I was too scared to ask. Thankfully, Dr G felt confident, so he asked everyone for me and made a plan. We went to Wagamama's and then spent the end of the evening with the last remaining people. It was a lovely, relaxed evening. We had breakfast with the South Wales guys the next morning, so it was nice to catch up and reminisce. The journey back was pleasant, and I absolutely loved it all.

Back home and a week later, we were in lockdown. Our event scheduled on 28th March had already been cancelled as a physical event, along with the rest of the regional groups in the hub. We held an online event for our community, and I also set up an online event channel on the main hub's server. The original rumours were that lockdown would be a few weeks at most, so we set up a schedule, and I started with a successful session of *Tetris99*, replicating what we did at the HQ visit. Fred streamed bits here and there too, but it was a bit of a half-hearted effort. After we realised the lockdown was getting more long-term, another founder offered to take over the schedule and started streaming regularly and consistently.

The third *Splatoon* tournament happened in 2020. It spread from May to August and had two tiers. This is what the previous tournament's survey had requested, so we delivered. This year I made the decision that we needed an organisational team. Fred and the original organiser fell out on the first day, so the original guy was nowhere to be seen for most of it. Fred kept telling people the wrong information and then making it look like it was my fault. During the whole tournament, we had a team of six. We had three additional volunteers: one was great, one was passive, and the other was a liability.

The higher league was first. These were the serious competitive ones. They moaned about the rules, there were racist slurs in some of the streams, and behaviour, although generally good, was overshadowed by those determined to act up. It culminated in a girl personally attacking me on the server. She tried to call me out over a misunderstanding that had come from her team not reading the rules thoroughly, and I got defensive too quickly. That was on me, but when my anxiety triggered, I would always react emotionally. My heart was pounding, I was shaking and had chills despite being hot outside, and I didn't sleep that night. Thankfully, it got sorted by Fred talking her team down. However, I later found out he'd told them more wrong information. On that occasion, I just appreciated that he'd shut them up. That was the end of May. I realised at that point, across all areas of my life, I needed to sort out my mindset. After the personal attack took me a couple of weeks to get over the trigger, it made me feel like a failure.

Over the next month, the lower league tier was in play, but behind the scenes, I was doing a lot of self-development. The lower league was equally a headache. People weren't happy that higher teams were in there. They thought it was a casual league. I did try to explain to them that there had to be a line drawn down the middle of the total entries, and you could also still be higher level but a casual player. For example, I didn't compete at all, but I was S+ rank at my peak, which is pretty high for a casual player.

There were rumblings throughout the whole thing, but at this point, I just wanted it to be over. There were two weeks left, and I'd had yet another row with Fred. It was mid-August 2020 when I finally gave up and simply said to Fred that I was done. I didn't elaborate, but in truth, I was truly done. Done with the community, done with the hub, done with everything. However, my heart and soul were still in it, even if at that point my mind wasn't. I knew it was my passion, and deep down, I wasn’t going to give it up for anything.

I waited for the *Splatoon* tournament to end and went back to the central admin with a cry for help. By coincidence, the passive admin said he was sorry he wasn't as involved as he could have been, so felt like he should step down. I messaged him straight away, "Election?! Let's re-haul the whole thing and do this properly!"

We took it back to the other two admin, and they backed it almost straight away. I informed the Nintendo Manager, Mack, about what we were doing, and he wished me luck. That was it, now or never! In September 2020, I found my 'roar'! I announced to the founders' group that we were calling an election. There was going to be a committee of eight: four panel admins, three for the social media team, and a head admin. Every place was available. All you had to do was fill in the Google form and submit a manifesto. Over the next few weeks, we went through the process and made sure it was as fair as possible. I ran it because I was seen as the one in charge already. My reputation of being honest, trustworthy and reliable didn't let me down. Fred accused me of backstabbing and went to Mack to complain, only for him to back me up instead.

The Tropic Product Launch had been a great but slightly anxious day, and I looked awesome in my Popsy Winona Windmill dress, having also trialled the Tropic makeup for the first time in real life. When I got back, it was time to reveal the election results. I changed into my Amber fireworks dress because I knew I'd got the Head Admin position. I went live into the group. No one had ever gone live in that group before. I felt confident and sincere. We'd won! There was a resounding yes all around. The four who applied for the panel got in, and three out of five won the social media positions. Everyone was happy that there was finally some direction and structure to the hub after all these years.

From September, I decided to have fortnightly committee meetings, where we could have accountability, keep each other up to date, and create action points to keep progressing. It's worked well so far, and there's been plenty going on to keep the hub and its communities busy. The new social media team increased engagement and reach ten-fold. Community members were commenting on what an astounding difference they'd noticed, and that was just after the first month.

Meanwhile, Fred had put a grand speech out that made him look like he was pushed out, but he chose to leave. The truth was we were forced to push him out because he was the centre of all the problems. But we were as transparent as possible, and it was a joint decision actioned by the four original admin, not by me alone.

We ran into slight hiccups earlier in 2021 when one of the admin panel left citing personal reasons, and no one quite knew why. Before I knew it, his partner started having a go at me on a thread, accusing me of creating a dictatorship. Thankfully this time, I had a committee to back me up, and it took me less than a day to recover mentally from the anxiety trigger she caused me. This time I didn't see myself as a failure. I knew that the self-development that I'd worked so hard on had paid off. The only thing left of my anxiety disorder to work on at that point was how to stop triggers from happening in the first place.

The fourth season of Squid League happened over the summer of 2021. For the first time, the lead tournament organiser was a different person—a streamer who was a competitive *Splatoon* player. The expertise was much needed, and the original guy was still in the background. I took a back seat and was on hand if she needed any assistance. It wasn't without its issues, though. People were quick to jump down each other's throats, and when the lead TO tried to change the layout of the final knockout stage, there was uproar. In the end, nothing changed. I was just relieved that I wasn't in the face of the drama this time. I was no longer weak, but she was coming from a more authoritative place as far as the game was concerned. We didn't envisage the toxic behaviour displayed by a certain team, which was egged on by the group's founder. As a committee, we'd been watching the founder in question since the spat earlier in the year, but we had no idea what we would experience.

I received a message late one evening from a hub member, saying they were being bullied live on stream. My committee was in a meeting at the time, so a few tuned in to hear it for themselves. In a word, it was horrific! I called an emergency committee meeting for the first time ever, and all members of the committee attended despite the short notice. The vote was unanimous to remove the community within the next twenty-four hours. We made sure everything was perfectly synched up, so they were removed from everything at precisely the same time.

The following day it was done. They were gone, with a formal email sent by me on behalf of the committee. They replied, denying everything and asking for evidence, but since most of the evidence was confidential, we couldn't divulge it. We outlined which rules they'd broken and reminded them of the hub's ethos. We heard nothing from them again via email. The next day they did a public stream and tried to insult every member of my committee. Yet the best insult they threw at me was, "She's such a dictator!"

I specifically told my committee to not react to anything. No matter how low the offending community stooped, they must not react. After that one stream, the community in question never spoke of any of it again in public. Mack, and other founders, commended us on how we dealt with the situation and congratulated us on our professionalism. That was the committee's proudest moment to date. No other drama has happened since then, we had another virtual get together for Christmas, and the hub is generally a feel-good and supportive place to be.

BECOMING A MAM

The Fear of Being Pregnant

2016 was an anxious year. But I didn't let it beat me. I felt stronger than I had the previous year, I was getting over the nightmare of the previous job, and I was enjoying the quieter life of just note taking and teaching the odd bit of piano. I was thirty that summer, and I was a little disappointed that most people couldn't make my birthday party, but Dr G surprised me, and eight of us had a little house party. I hated surprises, but I also kind of wanted one. I was convinced he'd forgotten right until that day, but when Ross drove a non-local friend to my house and dropped me off, I'd realised by then! It was a fantastic day, with great cake, but that was it. I'd hit my thirties. I was feeling happier about myself. I knew that my piano business would grow in time, so I focused on enjoying that summer.

It was the summer that Ross came to live with us, and it was also the summer of *Pokémon GO*! This involved lots of random little road trips chasing Pokémon whilst Dr G was at work. The summer holidays were always fairly jobless for me, but this year I made the most of it. It was the middle of August we decided to try for a baby. However, we didn't technically try; we decided to have a bit of fun instead. My anxiety told me that making life decisions was dangerous, so if I didn't make the decision myself, it was safer. This was one decision I didn't want to make. There was one problem with this. We never knew the date of conception. We used to joke it was the day Ross moved out, but in truth, we never actually knew.

I never thought about it either. I started my job as the sighted guide and worked right through Michael's degree, so he was on that entire journey with me. It was the first week we were properly working together, and I was late on my period. My periods were fairly predictable unless I was extremely stressed, but this was not one of those times. I'd just participated in freshers' week at the university, so I'd had a little bit to drink. One of the evenings around then, I went to see *Bridget Jones' Baby* with one of my community friends, Mia. We had pizza, and we watched the film. All the while, I was thinking, what if I'm pregnant.

The next day I purchased a pregnancy test. I got a cheap one, but I didn't believe it. I did it twice and still didn't believe it. I went out again and bought a Clear Blue test. 'Six weeks plus', it stated on the screen. I went into full panic mode then. I was also thinking that if I was going to have a baby, I should be ready now, but mentally I wasn't ready at all! Dr G was supportive but also very blunt. "You have two choices. You keep it, or you get rid."

I had to book an appointment with the midwife straight away. This was anxiety-inducing because I was frightened of doctors, waiting rooms, and anything associated with them. I was terrified when I walked into the room where there were two midwives. The older one was lovely, and the second one was still learning. I tried to stay calm. They talked me through everything and gave me various leaflets and books to read. They weighed and measured me. I was labelled obese and told to change my diet. I was fuming! I'd always been a bit overweight, but I wasn't obese. I had muscles. I got a bit emotional at that, but they managed to calm me down. At the end, they asked if I had any questions. I asked, "What happens if you eat swordfish?" having had some for tea the previous night. "Oh, I'm sure it won't do any harm, though no one has ever asked that before!" chuckled the older midwife.

Then came the 'you can't eat that' list, so the most memorable sacrifice was giving up liver, paté and soft cheese. I was gutted but so scared of doing something wrong that I cut out everything on the list. I had quite a healthy diet while pregnant, simply because I was so scared of putting a foot wrong.

I was terrified of being pregnant in general. I was freaking out inside with a million and one things that could go wrong. What if it killed me? What if it died? What if I had a miscarriage? Stillbirth? What if it was disabled or autistic? Anything could be wrong with it! The biggest fear was pre-eclampsia. I had all these thoughts going around my head, and it was a mess. I had an appointment with the mental health team, but they decided that because I refused the pills and had a decent family, I didn't need professional help, so they discharged me.

Thankfully at a similar time, I saw on a Facebook group that a CBT student was looking for guinea pigs, and I'd heard that CBT was beneficial, so I contacted her by email and asked if I could sign up. This was the best thing I could have done.

She was with me for just a term, but the weekly sessions were invaluable. She recommended me a book called *Mind over Mood,* and we worked through it together. Originally it was supposed to be about my Generalised Anxiety Disorder, but it ended up being specifically about managing the pregnancy since she saw how terrified I was. She began by suggesting I start a journal. That was one of the best things I did. Not only does it have all the memories for when I was most sleep-deprived, it genuinely helped me get through the worst bits and helped me to analyse and rationalise many of my fears. Another suggestion she had early on was invaluable too. "You said you had a supportive husband? Talk to him. Tell him your worries and just see what he says." The next day I did just that. In my journal, I wrote down every single fear I had about being pregnant. I read them to him one by one, and he answered them all. I wrote the answers down, and I found it comforting when I needed it throughout my pregnancy.

The pregnancy was almost too good. There was no sickness, no symphysis pubis dysfunction, and no extra pains except a bit of sciatica towards the end. Generally, I slept ok apart from maybe the last week or two. I had a smallish bump and a small baby. I later found out that the medication I was on before I was pregnant has a possible side effect on a baby's growth, so unless he catches up, I'll always wonder if it was my fault for not realising I was pregnant sooner.

The route with the professionals wasn't as smooth, though. Each blood test I had to have was traumatic. I had an awful fear of needles, and the first blood test caused massive bruising. Blood tests while pregnant are standard, so by the end, I'd got used to it. I had to have a pint of water and a bowl of soup before my appointment, so they had a chance of finding my veins. However, the GTT (*gluten tolerance test*) failed. I had to have that because I was marked as obese. They told me nil by mouth from the night before, but because I couldn't eat breakfast and was starving, dizzy and dehydrated, they didn't have a hope of finding my veins. I warned them, but they didn't listen. The test failed, and they told me I had to come back. I refused, and it went down in my notes as having refused second test.

I was sent to hospital a couple of times after a standard midwife appointment because my blood pressure was high. The medication I had to take while pregnant was less than ideal, as it was anti-hypertensive rather than beta blockers, so it had a different effect. My blood pressure was all over the place. It was like when you have an HP metre in a video game, and it kept sinking (pressure got higher) until you took the next one. I even had to have one of those days of the week pill boxes because I struggled to remember to take them three times a day.

In January 2017, I'd just had my twenty-week scan, so we found out the gender of the baby. The nub theory and other people's guesses suggested it was a girl, so I was convinced. I didn't mind, and I planned on gender-neutral clothes, but I had all girls' names in my head. Upon going to the scan, I was nervous, but Dr G was with me. There was a guy on duty that day. He did the scan and asked if I felt I knew what I was expecting, and I said girl. He zoomed in on my baby's penis, pointed towards it and said, "Nope, that's definitely a boy!" Dr G laughed! I didn't know whether to laugh, cry, or do nothing. I didn't feel anything. I now had to think of boys' names, though. We went home and went through all the (Welsh) boys' names I'd listed in my journal. There were about twenty girls' names and three boys' names. We ruled out two of them and were left with one. That was the one!

The week after the scan, we went to the Nintendo Switch premiere. I was anxious all day because it was a city, London, and I had to travel on a coach, but they saved me a seat at the front, and some knew I was pregnant too. I did well to last all day, as I was mainly on my feet. We got dropped off at Warrington, and I needed the toilet. The chain pub restaurant had just shut for the night, but I was pregnant and desperate, so I knocked on the door as they were locking up and explained I was pregnant. They let me in without any fuss. It was the exit that amused me. I came out of the building towards the car, and one of the guys from the group I was travelling with piped up and said, "How did you get in there?" "What do you mean?" I asked. "Did you use your pregnancy card?!" "What?" "The pregnancy card? Did you have to show it?" I couldn't stop laughing. I had to explain to him that pregnant ladies didn't carry around cards of declaration!

I went on a weekend away in February. I probably would have been twenty-five weeks pregnant by then. What I didn't expect was milk. No one warned me about that! I had no idea what it was at first and freaked out a little bit when we were in our room at the hotel. Dr G thought it was funny, and I think I just ended up wiping it and pretending nothing had happened. That was no warning to what it would be like having milk for real. That was a whole other league of hell I wasn't expecting.

By the March, I was heavily pregnant. I was the accompanist for the music society choir, and it was their spring concert. I could do my part, but I asked the conductor if he'd sort a page-turner out for when my co-accompanist was playing. On the night, it turned out they'd forgotten, so I was literally in the queue to go on stage when they said, "Jen, there's no page-turner. Can you do it? You know the pieces the best." I sighed and agreed. The 'Les Misérables Medley' was a nightmare. The accompanist went out of time to the choir halfway through it, so I had to try and conduct him back in. I was leaning across the piano to turn pages and was scared that my bump would get in the way of the piano. I was singing for bits of the concert too, so waddling across the stage was attractive, especially since it was on live stream and some watching (who knew me) only just realised I was pregnant!

For the overall pregnancy, I wanted as few people to know as possible. I told my close family, and that was it. Michael obviously knew, and his peers probably noticed. The interesting fact was that Dr G's colleagues weren't aware. They were also my ex-colleagues from maternity cover in 2014, but I didn't stay in touch with any of them because I'd never felt properly included. I told Dr G not to tell them initially. He told his closest colleagues, and I had to tell certain managers because I technically still worked for the same department.

There were specific reasons why my blood pressure kept spiking around the March. The Nintendo Switch had just been released, and I'd been playing the latest *Zelda* game, *Breath of the Wild*. Every time I lost against a Divine Beast, I would get stressed. There was a certain awkwardness of explaining that to a midwife who didn't know anything about gaming apart from, "I had a Nintendo Wii once!"

There was one particularly fateful day when my blood pressure was elevated again. I was sent to the hospital around lunchtime. What I didn't know was that I'd then get ignored by the staff and be stuck there for over eight hours without food or medication because they needed the registrar to sign me off. The registrar wasn't there for most of the day, as they were attending to emergency patients in another area of the hospital. I was too anxious to complain back then, so I just sat there quietly. Other patients came and went; I was still there at teatime. I was getting hungry, so Dr G asked if they would be much longer. They offered us some food, but I have to eat gluten-free, so the only thing they had to offer was an out-of-date yoghurt—I passed. I waited and waited. There was another pregnant lady there, equally fed up but also a bit more vocal. She'd accepted she might have to stay overnight, but all she wanted was a cup of ice.

It was 10 pm, and we were still there! I felt like I was going to keel over, and the other pregnant lady was still wanting her cup of ice. Dr G decided to grab us a McDonald's. I was past the point of caring about it being gluten-free. At that point, I was desperate. He remembered the lady's cup of ice too. We'd never been so relieved to eat. We finally got signed off at 11 pm, having been sitting there since 1 pm. I'd had a mini panic attack because I'd missed my medication. I didn't think to bring it with me because I expected to only be there for about half an hour. Ironically, they were keeping me in because of high blood pressure. I was getting stressed because they wouldn't listen, and I was trying to tell them I'd missed my medication and needed it to bring the blood pressure down. I was emotional, and I felt like they treated me like that silly little girl again. Finally, at 11 pm, we were allowed to go home. For someone who was terrified of hospitals, this majorly exacerbated my fears.

I knew I wanted to try hypnobirthing and hoped that I wouldn't have to have any intervention. I didn't even like water, but the people I'd spoken to on various forums convinced me that a water birth was the way forward. On my birthing plan, I wrote that I wanted a private room, and I would be hypnobirthing in a pool. I didn't want any intervention, and I only wanted a caesarean section if I was dying. I later realised that was both a stupid and dangerous thing to put because if I'd been taken for a C-section, I'd have gone into panic mode and been convinced I was dying. I submitted the plan, and nothing was said.

I was under a consultant because of my blood pressure. I think I met her once or twice. She was a sporty, no-nonsense character, and naturally, I was scared of her. She talked through my birthing plan and said she'd do what she could to help me. I was still terrified about the concept of pre-eclampsia. It wasn't causing regular panics either by that point, I generally kept myself busy, so I didn't have time to think about it. I did feel calmer after the first meeting, at least. She put on my notes that I'd need a private room, and I thought I was safe.

I was also warned by other mothers who'd been

through it that whatever your birth plan says, it probably wouldn't go that way. That was the worst thing an anxious pregnant lady could hear. I liked to have control of the situations I found myself in, so I was at the lowest risk of an anxiety attack.

One of Dr G's colleagues noticed me walking up the road in early May. It was two days before I gave birth. She told the rest of the office, and the cat was out of the bag. For special occasions, they liked to get gifts together for colleagues, so they scrambled something together at short notice but had a massive send-off for the one they knew about who had their baby at roughly the same time. I didn't mind, though. I didn't want them to know anyway.

Thanks to that academic year of working with Michael, I'd kept fit by doing ten-thousand steps pretty much every day as part of my job. I'd also been doing weekly Pilates classes since 2015 and seeing my sports rehab person once or twice a month. They all played a part in helping me be my best physical self, ready for childbirth. I believe without a combination of all the above, it likely wouldn't have gone as well as it did. I was still overweight, though, but at the same time, I hadn't put any weight on during my pregnancy.

My baby came three weeks early. I was supposed to see Michael off for the end of his first year. It was his final week of assessments, and I had to hand him over for his last few days. I was gutted, but I also knew that I couldn't multitask my job while giving birth! I did ask how he did a week later because I was concerned. The baby arrived so early I hadn't yet gotten around to reading how to do hypnobirthing, so I was trying not to panic, as I had no idea what I was doing.

I was so aware that pre-eclampsia could start around week thirty-seven that maybe it was a blessing in disguise. I never suffered from pre-eclampsia in the end. Was that because I delivered him in the thirty-seventh week? I'll never know. I just learnt to be grateful at that point.

People used to joke about being able to breathe through childbirth but would assume the mother would have gas and air, if not an epidural. However, I was so scared of intervention I was determined to give birth without any pain relief. The birth plan I'd written was ringing in my ears. 'No drugs, c-section or intervention'. The people in my life had told me that nothing goes to plan when it comes to childbirth.

That Tuesday, I'd walked eleven thousand steps as part of my job and then came home and randomly decided to wash my car, as it had bird muck all over it. It was 4 am on Wednesday, and I woke up thinking I'd wet the bed! I went to the toilet and thought, "Shit, that's my waters breaking!" I woke up Dr G, and he drove me to the hospital. They confirmed my waters had broken. I was only thirty-seven weeks, and I wasn't ready physically or mentally. I'd not had time to read the hypnobirthing book; I hadn't got a clue what I was doing, I hadn't even packed the hospital bag that everyone harped on about! The contractions were quite far apart at that point.

The next bit terrified me. The midwife was going to check how much I was dilated using a speculum. She failed because the rest of my waters came out. She confirmed it was definitely my waters but added, "If you haven't dilated enough within twenty-four hours, we'll have to induce you due to risk of infection." Nope. This is not happening, I thought to myself. They sent me home and told me to come back in twelve hours for checks. My husband was calm and helped me to stay calm. We told the people we needed to and then concentrated on being calm. We gathered the things I thought I needed. There were three bags. A baby bag, my holdall, and a bag of snacks and 'things to do'.

We actually had quite a normal day. I figured that if I stayed calm, the baby might arrive quicker, so when we got back home, I had a nap. There was a whole bulb of garlic in the fridge, and I decided that day I'd better chop it and freeze it before I forgot. My fingers stank of garlic after, but I quite like garlic, so it was almost comforting. It ended up playing a huge part in the actual childbirth too.

As requested, we returned to the hospital at 4.30 pm to be met with confused staff who didn't understand why we were called back in twelve hours rather than the typical twenty-four. They did the checks then sent us home again, telling me to return at 10.30 pm. We went home and had tea: fish fingers, mushy peas and alphabet potato shapes. We then went for a walk to see if it would speed up my contractions a bit. I remember they started to get a bit closer together, and we took in the moody sunset that evening as we were walking.

We arrived at the hospital later that night, and they'd put me in a bed by the window. It was a compromise, as they explained that I wouldn't be able to have a private room due to more urgent cases needing them. I looked around nervously but just had to make do. What I didn't realise is that no overnight guests were allowed. But Dr G was my birthing partner! "No, he's a guest. He has to leave now," stated the midwife. I got emotional, as I was being left on my own, but Dr G convinced me I'd be ok. They said he could return at 4.30 am as that was the twenty-four-hour mark. I was gutted.

Thankfully, I had my iPod and headphones. What I didn't bargain for was the dodgy internet. My iPod wouldn't connect, and I was relying on Spotify. I couldn't survive without music, and I needed it for my coping mechanisms. I also had an iPhone 7, so I used that instead. But it only lasted until 2 am, and then the battery died. The design problem with more recent iPhones was that you couldn't charge it by cable as well as plug in headphones. All I had was a dock. My contractions were five minutes apart. I was starting to get anxious. I was too scared to get up and ask for help in case I disturbed someone. I was getting desperate, so eventually I managed to flag down a member of staff who was passing by, and ask her if there was somewhere more private I could go. She asked some colleagues, and they found me a treatment room that I could camp out in. I grabbed my iPhone, dock and plug and went straight there. I didn't realise until later that I had left all my snacks by my bed in the ward.

That treatment room was where I did the main part of the labour. Alone with just a tap, a plastic cup for water, a gym ball, the treatment bed, and my music. Apparently, that's all I needed, but I was completely alone. My birthing partner had been sent home, I had no help, and every couple of hours, a member of staff would come to get something from the room, remember I was in there and ask if I was ok. I always said I was fine. I was not in a private room and completely on my own, but I was fine. I could handle the pain.

I learnt to deep breathe through pain thanks to the lady I'd been having sports rehab from, as well as resources from my Pilates teacher. Between those experiences, I essentially breathed and did Pilates throughout the labour. Not forgetting that every time I breathed in, I smelled pungent garlic, and I wondered on reflection if that's why I forgot to eat.

They told me to call them when my contractions were three minutes apart, but they seemed to have forgotten about me. I managed to get someone's attention, and she said she would be back in a minute and disappeared. It felt like forever until she came back. It was definitely a lot longer than a minute. It felt like hours! It was nearly 4.30 am by that point, so I was starting to go into panic mode. I didn't want a pessary. I didn't want any intervention. Thankfully, Dr G reappeared at that point, but my contractions were two minutes apart by then and were getting ridiculously painful. They kept offering me gas and air, and even though I was struggling, I still refused it. They refused to examine me until the twenty-four hours had passed, which dragged like hell! Dr G was useless until the actual birth, as he was too late for the first stages.

This was when things started to go wrong. I couldn't be on my back as I had chronic back pain before I was pregnant, which made it worse. Yet, to examine me, they forced me onto my back. I wanted to be on all fours, but they kept forcing me onto my back. I was going into panic mode! In the end, they seemed to understand and held the monitors underneath me so I could be on all fours again. It's safe to say my huge list of pieces from my *Piano in the Background* playlist, plus having garlic hands and a gym ball, is what got me through childbirth when nothing else did.

Right towards the end, they got me on my back and realised I was 5 cm dilated, and they almost went into panic mode themselves. I'd been trying to tell them I was ready, but they wouldn't listen until they'd checked by measuring. At that moment, they realised I should be in the labour ward! As they "undressed" me and wheeled me to the labour ward, I felt like I had to "pause" my delivery because I wasn't in the "right" room! They still kept offering me gas and air, but even though I was wavering and starting to think I couldn't do it, I still refused. My body told me to push, but my brain told me we were in the wrong room.

We finally made it to the delivery suite. I was paranoid about leaving my stuff in the ward, and all I had with me was my phone, dock, and headphones. Dr G plugged my dock in so the piano music could continue. I was on all fours, optimum position, and the next thing I knew, the midwives were telling me to stop pushing! I couldn't stop; my body had taken over, and I just wanted to push! They shouted at me to stop pushing, but I couldn't. They even told me off for not listening! They said his pulse was dropping, so I went into panic mode! I was killing my baby! Eventually, I managed to hold back a push, and I engaged my brain. Then I let out the loudest roar Dr G had ever heard, and that was it, my baby was out!

This tiny baby was crying, but he quickly became quiet. He was quite happy, perched on my chest. I felt bad, though. His cord had to be cut earlier than we would have liked, as it was so short, he couldn't reach my breast. There was a tiny bit of humour, too, as Dr G was given the chance to cut the cord, but the midwife had to guide his hand, so he didn't chop the tiny boy's willy off! Meanwhile, they had to give me an injection to get the placenta out, as I was losing too much blood. I was still in pain from the initial birth, so I barely noticed it.

As soon as the cord was cut, my baby latched on straight away but was too sleepy after just a few minutes. Dr G got some skin-to-skin time with him while I got stitched up. I had a second-degree tear, but apparently, it was going the other way to what was expected. That was a nightmare, as the midwife trying to stitch me up kept telling me to relax, but my legs had turned to stone. I was so tense. Even though she'd numbed the area, it still hurt.

My baby was here. A dark mop of hair, at 5lb 11oz, 5.50 am.

It was shortly after that I realised I hadn't eaten for the whole of labour. I only realised when I tried to stand up. There's never been a weirder sensation than realising you're going to faint. I sat back down before I fainted. I don't know how I managed. It was an out of body experience, that's for sure. I'd just missed the breakfast request, so I got a special order instead. I asked for gluten-free bacon butties and savoured every bite.

I was there for a while, and the midwives had swapped shifts. I ended up being wheelchaired to the postnatal ward, as I couldn't walk. I requested the bed by the window again since I couldn't have a private room. A bit later in the morning, I tried to have a shower. I just about made it into the shower, but I couldn't dress afterwards. I went into panic mode, as there was no way I was leaving the shower without any clothes on. I remember putting my sleep bra and nighty on, stepping outside the shower room and scaring the student midwife as I nearly collapsed in front of her. A more senior midwife noticed and jumped forward to help me to stay on my feet.

There were a couple of hours for visitors in the afternoon, so the parents all visited, except the father-in-law, who was working the elections that day. Even my brother made it up to the hospital. Everyone took a photo with the baby. It was a nice couple of hours, but I was a bit tired, so I sat there spaced out. Dr G had used that chance to nip home and grab some bits. When he returned, I was pretty out of it, so he used the time to learn everything about the baby. He had a go at everything with a bit of help from the midwives. I was just staring blankly into space for most of it. A member of staff taught me how to express milk using a knitted boob as a prop, and she helped me collect the first bits of colostrum.

When it came to kicking out time for overnight guests, I became emotional. I didn't want to be left alone with my baby, but they wouldn't listen and sent Dr G home again. I tried to occupy myself by talking to people on Facebook or writing my journal, but I was exhausted, eventually becoming too tired to hold anything. I attempted to go to sleep, but it was impossible. Two new babies in the ward were crying or screaming most of the night. My baby was quiet and was due a feed every three hours, so I was almost too scared to fall asleep, but I managed to grab an hour at midnight.

An hour's sleep in forty-eight hours was not good. I was struggling to feed him too, so the midwives tried to help, but every feed, he spat it out or threw it up. I ran out of baby grows and had to change the sheets three times. At 2 am, the midwife discovered he'd done a poo, probably a while ago, and asked why hadn't I noticed? I felt like a failure as a mother, and it was less than twenty-four hours in. I sent a Facebook message to Dr G at 3.20 am. I knew he was asleep, so he'd read it when he woke up, but it said, 'I'm fed up, I'm exhausted, and I feel completely useless.' I then got emotional when a midwife popped her head around my curtain. She asked if I wanted to talk, so I told her, through tears, how I felt. A mum on the other side of the ward complained to another midwife that I was making too much noise.

After the talk, I managed to get one more hour of sleep. My anxiety was sky-high. My limbs had gone stiff, the bed was uncomfortable, and I felt completely useless and fed up! The baby then did a loud poo, so at least I noticed that time, but I panicked. I pressed the red button, but no one came. I muddled through it on my own and messed up the whole thing. A midwife did come and help eventually. It turned out the plug for the button had fallen out of the wall when I'd dropped it earlier in the night.

The morning was ok. I was assuming I'd be going home, but by 11 am, I'd learnt I wasn't going home. I was devastated and sobbed. A second midwife came to talk to me, and she offered me three options: walk around premises, use a private room, or chill in the café, then come back. I insisted that I needed to go home. It was sleep I needed, not fresh air! I sobbed more. They suggested Dr G could come back earlier, but it was only half an hour until he was due anyway, so that was pointless. When he turned up, I cried all over him. We had lunch together, so by then, I calmed down a bit.

The paediatrician came by to examine my baby and advised that he needed to be moved to the special unit. He said I had to stay in the ward, which stopped me in my tracks. "What?!" I cried. Why should I stay in the ward when my baby wasn't even with me?! It was at this point I was starting to lose it completely. I threatened to abandon my baby. I had complete control of my thoughts, but I felt like I was being ignored, so I thought of the one thing that would force them to listen.

A third midwife appeared, giving me the three options again. I repeated the same answer I gave to the second midwife. Eventually, she agreed that I would be better off at home. I breathed a huge sigh of relief. She gave me the paperwork to sign, so I could discharge myself. It was like I had a new lease of energy. I stopped feeling like a dark cloud was over me.

I packed up my stuff as Dr G took my baby over to the special unit. He didn't come back, though, so the midwife took me over to the unit, and I was able to see my baby before I left him to go home. He was fast asleep and looked perfectly content, and I wasn't concerned about him at all. All I wanted was sleep. Just before I left the hospital, the original student midwife came to see me to ask if I was ok. I was deliriously happy at that point, so she said she could see I was fine and seemed more confident than previously. As soon as I got home, I slept for the rest of the afternoon until it was time for tea.

My baby spent one week in the special unit. We visited every night to feed him, and I had to express during the day and breastfeed when we were physically there. That week, I just wanted to sleep and recover physically. It took about ten days for my stitches to heal, and the week my baby was in the special unit, we worked out that he was just waiting for my milk to be ready. My milk came in after three days, and he was ready then. The special unit kept him for the whole week to make sure I could look after him properly.

The fifth night we stayed over in a private ward room to get used to being around him more. The final night they set up a camp bed for Dr G so we could stay in the mother and baby special unit room so that we could get on-hand help, but we were solely in charge of looking after him from that point. I felt like I was being tested—pass this exam, and you'll get to take your baby home. I was anxious throughout the whole thing, but we survived. The unit made us feel supported. They were wonderful!

I can't say the same about the rest of the experience. I was ignored consistently to the point of which I had a breakdown a day after I gave birth. The irony was being told to write a thank you card and putting 'sorry for being noisy and talking your ear off'. When in fact, I was having a nervous breakdown.

That first week after the birth, the hospital was also closely monitoring my blood pressure, as it kept rising. I was also aware that the higher it went, the more likely I'd be back in hospital. I was terrified about that, so was determined to bring it down, but it wouldn't budge. I was overwhelmed and stressed, but even more stressed because

I felt watched. After lots of back and forth, they agreed to let me go home, as long as I monitored it every day. I couldn't wait to get back on my original medication. The medication through pregnancy just didn't work. I guess that's the difference between antihypertensives and beta blockers. I suppose the beta blockers helped with anxiety too. I had to wait until I'd finished expressing four months after the birth before I could go back on my original medication. It was hell. Upon returning to the original medication, I was put on a double dose because my blood pressure still wouldn't come down. I'm fortunate that as of February 2021, I was able to half that and come back to the original dose I was on when I first got diagnosed.

Those sleepless nights marred the first two years of being a mum. The first twelve weeks were the hardest. You know becoming a parent is supposed to be hard, but this was way beyond anything I could have dreamt of. Imagine having to breastfeed as well as express. Hardly any sleep for three months straight, trying to remember how to keep yourself alive, keep the house going, not to mention keeping a tiny baby alive. My brain didn't cope very well at all. To be fair, neither did Dr G's! I wasn't ready when the baby was born. I wasn't ready after he was born either. I'd read the books, but nothing made sense. We had a lot of help from both sets of parents, but everything was a blur.

The first time we let the baby stay overnight at the grandparents' house, he was two weeks old. We'd maybe had about five hours of sleep for the whole two weeks, it was ridiculous. It may have been normal, but I quickly learnt that my entire mental health stability depended on sleep.

I was pressured into breastfeeding. I never wanted to, but I didn't have the guts to tell people that. I kept quiet because I felt judged. I felt selfish for not wanting to. Even my husband made me feel guilty. I didn't get a choice at the hospital. They assumed I would. They taught me how to do it, then sent me on my way. It was a month of pure hell. They said my milk would come in soon. It came in on day three. Not a single person had told me about the pain. It was agony. That on top of trying to recover 'down there'. There were a lot of tears, in addition to the issue of breastfeeding and expressing. I had to do both. It had its advantages because it meant Dr G could do some of the night feeds to help me get some sleep. The only problem was if the baby was awake, so was I.

I only complained to Dr G, but I hated every second of breastfeeding. It was painful, often agony. Being engorged was pure hell too. However, I admit it had funny moments seeing how far it would go in the shower. I felt like I'd lost my identity. I was just some cow with udders. I had to express every four hours and feed every three hours. It was just unrealistic, and I only lasted a single month breastfeeding. I couldn't take the pain anymore. I lasted four months with the expressing. We got to three months, and Dr G agreed I should stop as he could see what it was doing to me, but we couldn't just stop, we had to wind it down. It took a month, going from every four hours to every twenty-four hours. It was a weekend in Newcastle that marked when I wished to stop by.

Mastitis is usually the biggest concern for breastfeeding. I was sitting on my own with my baby one afternoon. At 2.50 pm, I was fine. Suddenly at 3 pm, I had flu! It hit me just like that. I panicked, and of course, it had to be a

Thursday afternoon, so my local doctor's surgery was closed. I had to drive to the sister surgery for an urgent appointment. As soon as I got the flu symptoms, I went into panic mode and was shaking like a leaf through the whole experience. It was a quiet surgery, but what I didn't bargain for was running into my least favourite doctor from my home surgery and him telling me off for calling cystitis an emergency. I clearly said mastitis on the phone. They're two completely different things, and the latter, if left untreated, could lead to death! I was terrified, and the doctor made me cry in frustration. I had to wait for the dispensary to release my antibiotics, though, so I managed to calm down before I had to leave. How I drove there and back on my own, I'll never know. I'm pretty sure I wasn't safe to drive that day. The mastitis cleared up with medication. After a week, I was aware that the trigger for my mastitis was a day out in Chester without Dr G. I'd tried to express on my own and made a mess. I learnt my lesson. Don't go and express without Dr G's assistance.

The first three months of a child's life are the hardest. I know plenty of couples split up around this time, and I can understand why. The less sleep we had, the more argumentative we got. Dr G and I had never been deprived of sleep before, let alone for long periods of time. It's true you forget about the birth and the baby bit. My baby's entire first two years are just a weird haze. Maybe that's why people go and have another one. I am never doing this again, and I won't forget because I journaled the whole thing.

I only had the legal two weeks off for maternity leave. Having only gone self-employed the year before and being on a zero-hours contract for everything else, I wasn't entitled to anything. I didn't want maternity leave anyway. A year off with your kid sounded like a nightmare! I had the two weeks off then went straight back into it. It sounded harder than it was because I already worked from home, so all I had to do was email my small handful of piano students and tell them they could come back.

Dr G's parents were the main childcare. There was a great support network, and my parents started visiting once a fortnight too. My mum would stay over whenever Dr G's parents were away on holiday.

I journaled every single day. I was usually expressing at the time, but it helped me cope. I tracked his progress, and I put down appointments, jabs, and how we were feeling. It was really useful. The breaking point happened at about three months in, though. We were both losing the plot completely. We were taking turns to get up for the baby, but some nights he wasn't sleeping at all. One night, Dr G was ready to cry. He just dumped the Moses basket in the landing and stormed off. I took that as my sign to take over again. We needed help! Thankfully, the baby was able to stay over at Dr G's parents' house when we were desperate.

On the outside, we carried on as normal. Dr G had a month off work, as he used both paternity leave and some annual leave. I dreaded him going back to work, but I didn't have a choice. I got back into my Pilates classes as soon as I could, but often, I'd not remember how I got there. The other ladies once told me I looked dead! I felt like a zombie for several months, I don't know how we survived, but we did.

I went to the local baby and mum class when he was a

newborn, but my social anxiety often got the better of me, and I failed to make lasting friendships simply because I was too afraid to call people outside of the sessions.

Twelve weeks was the benchmark. People told me that once that benchmark was passed, we were on the home stretch. Nope. We were sleep-deprived for two years. My mental health dipped often, but we had our community meets to look forward to once a month, where we could just be Dr G and Jen again, if only for a day. Our monthly games nights turned to quarterly, but that wasn't a bad thing, it made them more special and something to look forward to. We kept things as normal as we could, but the truth was our relationship was suffering. It almost reached breaking point in 2019.

Every time my little boy went through a developmental phase or teething, he wouldn't sleep. Every time he had a cold, he'd get so blocked up, he'd have coughing fits, so we'd have to administer an inhaler and lie with him all night. That floor was cold and hard in the middle of the night. Memories of wrapping up in a dressing gown, fleece blanket, using a beanbag as a pillow at 4 am and being on a rota with Dr G to make sure we were sharing the duties as much as possible.

As a family, we have a happy little boy, and he wants for nothing. I bonded with him after about four months, but even though I didn't bond with him in those first few months, I still took all those pictures and wrote in my journal. I even started a blog for him that I update every single month. I never didn't care or love my child, I just had to find my identity again and work out where I fitted in in the world. I look back at the journal entries and photographs now, and it still makes me emotional that I don't really remember that bit of his life, but I'm also grateful that even at my lowest mental health points, I still kept the memories.

Sleep deprivation affects everything, not just your mental health. It has physical effects and can mess all sorts of things up. I couldn't even have caffeine; I was living off sugar. My blood pressure medication increased, and I was a mess right up until I ended up in hospital in September 2019.

THE YEAR EVERYTHING STARTED TO CHANGE

2019 was the start of everything else. It was a bad year for my mental health, but I was no longer officially sleep-deprived. Mums in my networking groups often talk about losing their identity, but I'd struggled hard to keep it since day one. The simple reason was being aware that I'd wasted my younger years in fear of what people thought of me and, in turn, had been too scared to do anything. I had my successful community, but that was a team effort. It wasn't my success. I still felt like a failure. I felt like a crap mum, wife, and just about everything, really. I often had low moods, but I kept going as my piano students were quite plentiful, and I did enjoy teaching most of them. However, the more difficult or younger ones required me to be more awake, so because I couldn't have caffeine, I'd rely on sugar. I never went overboard. I'd have one chocolate bar a day or a piece of cake. It was getting to the point where I'd start eating a second chocolate bar or a handful of sweets to stay awake for the next lesson. I knew full well that the sugar crash half an hour later would sink my mood even more, so I got stuck in a vicious cycle.

Michael graduated that summer. We were ecstatic. It was a major triumph for him as a student and me as his assistant. He'd faced so much adversity, and we'd fought his corner so hard that year. We were relieved it was over and sad we were parting ways. While working with him, I was also his 'walking taxi' so I got my exercise in at my job. When he left, I was down to one job being a piano teacher. I didn't even consider fitness, and I didn't think to adjust my diet either. It was quite common for me to nip to the local supermarket's hot deli counter, as their breaded chicken was delicious. My brain didn't get the message that you have to adapt to your surroundings, so by the end of the summer holidays, I was the largest I'd ever been. I was a size sixteen, feeling sorry for myself, still scared of everything and everyone. I was living off sugar to stay alert.

A new term started. I wasn't energised about it; I was just indifferent. I used to have a chocolate stash. A whole cupboard full of all my favourite chocolates. I was hoarding Terry's Dark Chocolate Oranges because they were my absolute favourite. I was good at saving them, but once I'd open one, it took a lot of willpower not to eat the whole thing in one go. I'd only ever have three or four pieces at a time, until one day in mid-September. I was depressed and feeling sorry for myself. My anxiety was high, and there wasn't even a specific trigger.

I was waiting for my next student, and for some reason, I mindlessly ate half a chocolate orange. That might not seem bad to some, but this was in addition to monthly pub visits, not caring what I ate in general, and a varied but not great diet. I ate all the junk food at social occasions, and of course, I'd been relying on sugar for over two years since my little one was born. I was aware of diabetes risks, but I had no idea what was about to happen.

I'd had heartburn a couple of times over the summer holidays. It was agony, but it settled again. On reflection, I should have taken these as warning signs that I needed to change, but I didn't. I just suffered all night, moaned the next day, then went back to normal. I even bought some Gaviscon in case it happened again. But that day in September was another level. I was fine until the evening. Then through the night, I got the worst heartburn. My anxiety told me I was having a heart attack, but I didn't know what it was. After a few minutes, it wasn't around the heart, it was more towards the abdomen, but it was agony. The next three or so days, I continued in agony, but I was that scared of hospitals I wouldn't call them. I just lay on the sofa, barely able to eat or move. I managed watery porridge for tea, but that was it. I started googling my pains and thought I had appendicitis and would die.

I eventually rang the doctor and went to an appointment, but they referred me to the hospital. I was stuck there for the rest of the afternoon while they tried to work out what was wrong with me. They ruled out appendicitis. I'd had to cancel all my piano students, and I remember being super apologetic and feeling like I'd let them down.

I'd brought my Nintendo Switch to the hospital and played *Tetris* to pass the time whilst waiting. They came back and told me I had sludge in my gallbladder, as well as large gallstones. The gallstones themselves weren't a problem, but the sludge was. It was a build-up of all the rubbish I'd been eating over time. They kept me a bit longer to tell me that I needed to have my gallbladder removed. I went into panic mode. The concept of any type of intervention from a hospital terrified me. No way were they taking my gallbladder out! They went away and talked to a consultant. Eventually, they let me go, telling me I had to change my lifestyle and I might get away with it. They also booked me in for a review the following February.

When I arrived home, I had a breakdown. I was a failure. I had a food problem and didn't know how to fix it. Dr G comforted me but also didn't know what to say. The pain and symptoms lasted two weeks, so I had to eat very bland things and small amounts. However, every cloud has a silver lining! It takes roughly two weeks to lose the sugar cravings, and I was forced into it. I then became scared of eating the wrong things, so I dropped most sugar and fat and started drinking cider vinegar mixed with a small amount of apple juice, as I was told cider vinegar could help flush out the sludge. In those next few weeks, I lost quite a bit of weight. I was so anxious about everything that not only was I eating less, but I was also worrying myself thin. I did start buying fresh fruit and tried to plan meals, so I ate less red meat and more fish or chicken.

A month later was when the real change started to happen. *Ring Fit Adventure* came out on Nintendo Switch. In the Wii days, I loved *Wii Fit* and *EA Active*, but the novelty had worn off long ago. I joined gyms and quit them. However, I was still going to weekly Pilates classes four years later. I had my core muscles, but it wasn't enough to truly tone up. *Ring Fit Adventure* was brilliant. I got into it straight away and played it five days a week right up until lockdown.

It was the same month that I discovered a local mums networking group, MIB Anglesey. I ventured to a local pub restaurant and met the group for the first time. I was nervous and awkward, and my kid was causing havoc. He stole someone's toast, threw menus at one lady, and made noise all the way through the guest speaker's talk. At the same time, the group was really friendly and welcoming and didn't seem bothered by my kid. I returned every month after that but would sort childcare out, so I could hear the guest speaker and be less stressed. It was around this time that I met a few ladies that would go on to change my life in 2020, including a local Tropic Ambassador. I would always stay for lunch and have ham, egg and chips with a coconut sorbet for dessert, and I'd always have at least one or two people to talk to. However, I always felt nervous and awkward. I bought a small item from the Tropic lady as a way to make a connection. She was interested in the gaming side for her boys too. We kept in touch. I also connected with a lady called Joan, who later became the local network's leader, but at this time, it was also her first event.

By February 2020, I'd kept consistency with my diet and *Ring Fit Adventure*. I lost just over two stone and was the lightest I'd ever been as an adult. However, I was still in a really low place mentally. I was scared of everyone. The marker of that was mid-February. Dr G and I had decided to go to my favourite ice cream place, except we'd delayed to the Sunday because it was raining on the Saturday. We found out a few friends had gone the day before, and we hadn't been invited. I was gutted and couldn't understand why we hadn't been invited. I felt like I'd done something to upset the group of friends, and I became even more anxious. The following weekend was one of our community events. I was the host, so I had to interact a bit, but the clique that sat around one table were supposed to be my closest friends, yet I was scared of them. I didn't say a word to them unless it was admin related. The thought of trying to start a conversation with one of them sent shudders down my spine, yet I couldn't work out why I was feeling like that. It had been building over months, and I couldn't seem to get rid of it. We'd heard about Covid-19, but it wasn't that. Lockdown wasn't going to be announced for a few weeks. Looking back, it could have been anything that triggered me in the first place. That was the problem with Generalised Anxiety Disorder.

The Pandemic Years

I'd never heard of the word lockdown until it was used for the first time in my life in March 2020. In real life, I had all the anxiety that had been building up since approximately Autumn 2019, and it was just getting worse. That last community event in February left me feeling abandoned by those I thought were closest. I'd just been to visit Nintendo HQ the week before lockdown hit, and before we knew it, everything beyond 23rd March was cancelled. We were told to stay at home, and staying at home became law by the 26th March. It was good timing, as it was only one week before the Easter holidays, so I had time to gather my thoughts. Everything got cancelled. Big concerts, conventions, even the Olympics!

However, it was the first week in March I saw this coming. I was terrified. I knew my business as a piano teacher could go down the pan just like that, so I started to panic. I attended what was to be the last physical MIB Anglesey event and met another Tropic lady. I sat next to her for most of the meeting and loved her bubbly character and positivity. I wished I could be more like that. I met some others that day who have provided invaluable support ever since too.

It was that day that I decided to become a Tropic Ambassador. I'd looked into network marketing before, and as a student, I'd wanted to be a Body Shop at Home consultant but knew I'd never have the guts to host parties or be a salesperson. So what was different this time? I still didn't think I had the courage, but I also knew I needed something to focus on. When the piano stuff was low, what was I going to do? I signed up two days later, except I signed up with the first lady. I felt it wouldn't be fair to connect with her and sign up with the second one.

I didn't have a clue what I was doing, but I figured that anything new was better than what I was doing. My leader was encouraging, but I was still in an anxious hole. I spent the first month being overwhelmed and wondering how on earth I would get sales. What had I signed up for? I liked the discount rate and wanted to try the products myself. I had been into premium skincare since I'd planned my wedding and had used Elemis and Clinique for several years. The pull of Tropic was that it was natural, effective, cruelty-free and vegan. It also worked out at better value than what I had been buying previously. The more I learnt about it, the more I loved it. I loved that every purchase went towards funding world schools. I loved the history of the company and the background of its founder. It was all perfect! I set up my social media but wasn't expecting such a frosty response.

A lot of friends turned their noses up at the sound of MLM (multi-level marketing). Others declined to support me because they didn't use products, or they were a soap and water person. Every 'no' hurt, and the more nos I received, the more depressed I got. I was going to fail at this too. Everyone else who started had friends and family to support and buy from them. I was struggling to get anyone to take notice. I ended up constantly comparing myself to others, being even more terrified of being judged, and felt useless. We had team calls twice a week, and being the consistency queen that I was, I turned up to all of them. I can't remember how far in it was, a couple of months at most, and I made a comment about one of the other girls. She was doing really well, and I said, "Oh, she must have too much time on her hands!" She took personal offence, and I didn't realise the seriousness of the comment, as I'd made it as an off-the-cuff remark. I was told to apologise, and that immediately triggered my anxiety. I felt so guilty as I realised the implications of what I'd said. I did apologise. It was accepted, and we had a chat there and then. There was another meeting where the host had told me off for saying "I'll try" and corrected me to "I will", but I found that difficult and didn't understand why she felt the need to correct me.

It was at that point I took a look at myself and thought, this can't go on. It was towards the end of May, and I'd had problems in the UK section of the gaming community, which resulted in me having a breakdown. The start of June was the start of everything else. After a bit of a rubbish giveaway in my Facebook group, where the person won, and then I never heard from them again, I was a bit desperate, so I gave away a massive prize in my birthday month. My oldest, supportive friend, Ian, won it, which was awkward and awesome. Even though he didn't technically want to win it, I appreciated that I knew he wouldn't disappear.

Meanwhile, I'd moved my piano lessons online. I'd lost two-thirds of my students, but we made do with what we had. The support from those that stayed kept me going, but I also knew I could keep going because I had a side hustle that I could concentrate on.

I'd only set up my private Facebook group in April, a few weeks after setting up my public social media, as I realised that the group had so many more possibilities. I knew that being part of network marketing wouldn't mean I would become a success overnight. I wasn't naïve when I started, but I also had no direction.

At the end of April, two significant things happened. I decided to record a programme of piano music to post in my group. It took me all day to record because I was such a perfectionist. If I made one mistake, I had to start again. In the end, I was too stressed, so my husband said just post it. I did just that, and although I can hear every single mistake. However, those who viewed it loved it, and I got amazing feedback. A lesson was starting to get through to me. Is being a perfectionist worth it?

Secondly, I won a strategy call in one of my friend's groups. I was the top contributor for that month. Once I joined a group, I would always do my best to be active. Kelly is a social media manager, and I'd followed her and her incredible venture from when I'd met her at one of my earlier local networking meetings. I had the call in early May. It was the best session I could have had. She presented me with a strategy, which was simple but effective. Consistency is key. Always have a plan. Schedule ahead.

I went away from that session and have had a strategy ever since. I was always good at being consistent and diligent, so I channelled that into my new business. I scheduled my posts every week in advance. I learnt how to use Canva properly, and I signed up for various social media training, challenges, masterclasses, and talks. There would be some weeks where I'd have three things on the go, but I was so hungry to learn I kept doing them. Some weeks I did get overwhelmed, though.

I'd been networking consistently from the start of lockdown, but as the months advanced, I learnt how to network. I slowly branched out from my immediate local network and started joining other groups and networks.

At the end of May, I linked up with a lady who ran Resilience Voyage. We talked, and she asked if I'd be willing to share my story on their blog. I've always loved writing, but except for a few gaming articles, I'd never written anything publicly on another subject, let alone myself. I agreed enthusiastically but was also anxious. What if people read it and realised how much of a failure I was? What if people laughed at me? What if my family read it and judged me, or even worse, disowned me? She asked me if I'd be willing to write eight thousand words. I gasped; that seemed a lot! It was voluntary, but I was so used to doing things voluntarily I never even considered that. I was just happy to help. If sharing my story inspired others, it was worth it.

I started writing and didn't stop. Eight and a half thousand words and I kept it as concise as I could. I shared it, and she loved it. It wasn't published until the August, but I asked that only my first name be on it, just in case the 'wrong' people found it. I was still terrified of judgement.

I carried on networking. I came across another networking group that was fairly local, and from there, I met all sorts of other people, including the handful that were part of my main journey.

The Vision Board Queen did a talk in one of my original network group's meetings. She ran her own networking group, but it only appeared in the summer, so I joined her and her Vision group. Since my school days, I'd never had a vision or made goals. The sheer concept sent shudders down my spine. What if I failed like I had so many times before? What if people laugh at me? What if people try to ruin everything?

June was a pretty good month. I'd got over the drama from the *Splatoon* tournament, and it was my and Dr G's birthdays. I usually plan a house party for our joint birthday celebrations, but of course, that was cancelled. I was already convinced my birthday would be crap, but my husband surprised me by putting on a virtual party for me on *Animal Crossing New Horizons*. It was exactly what I was hoping for. Some of the friends who'd disappeared at the start of lockdown appeared, and briefly, I felt loved, but after the weekend, everyone vanished again. I was also really happy because my Tropic leader had started a story on my Facebook profile, and others added to it. It was exactly what I'd hoped for. I was so used to people just not caring, so it was nice to feel slightly cared about for once. I didn't feel like everyone hated me for the first time in quite a while.

I signed up for various training and self-development opportunities throughout lockdown. There was barely a week that I wasn't doing some kind of challenge or training. The summer holidays were always quiet for work, but they also gave me that extra bit of focus that I needed.

I also started going live in my group—on 8th May 2020. I did my first random prize draw. I was terrified, but I survived, and I got a buzz after it. It was that month I started going live regularly, doing a Thursday Lunchtime Live from 14th May onwards. I'm still doing that today. Around that time, I came across another Tropic lady, not in my team but fairly local. Angie had posted in one of the higher groups about plodding along, and I felt the same. She got scolded by the upline and told to think more positively, but for people like us, we can't just flick a switch. I messaged her, and we added each other. We've been friends ever since. What I learnt at this point was that we should acknowledge our negatives/failures and celebrate the wins. Acknowledging the negatives is an important part of the process, but not everyone is willing to do that.

I know that overall, I was lucky because my child was only just three, so he didn't need home schooling, it was all about learning through play, but I also felt guilty that I wasn't giving him my full attention. I needed to work. That summer, I was getting desperate for income, as I'd lost several thousands of pounds thanks to lockdown and being part of the gig economy. The government offered Self-Employed income Support (SEISS), but due to my business only being four years old and barely turning a profit until the most recent year, which wasn't counted, they paid me such a small amount it didn't make any difference. I couldn't stop spending. My money was tied to my mental health more than I realised.

In late June, I spotted Joan wearing a really nice dress that was casual enough but also pretty. I asked where she got it from, and she invited me to the community. I discovered that Popsy did music-themed dresses, so I was sold! I got all the musical dresses and realised the founder did weekly Sunday evening lives. Over the summer, before I knew it, I had approximately twenty dresses. Previously I'd been wearing jeans and black t-shirts all the time, so that summer, most of my wardrobe changed. I started wearing Popsy dresses every time I went live and shared a selfie on my Instagram to add a bit of a personal touch to it. I started getting more engagement, but it was small. One or two watched my lives, and sometimes I'd be talking to myself, but someone would always catch me on the replay, so it encouraged me to keep going.

Every time an incentive was thrown in for Tropic, I would panic. I wanted it, but I couldn't rely on my customers at that point because I simply didn't have enough regular customers. I wasn't completely without. One or two bought things fairly regularly, so I didn't mind putting in a bit myself since I was technically a customer too. There was a fine line between buying what I needed and buying for the sake of it, though. I did this with the headband and water bottle. When it got to later in the year, I skipped the cooler and the diary, as I just knew that they were out of reach. I wanted to concentrate on building my customers and relationships rather than being desperate for sales, so it was at this point my mindset started to change.

It was also around late summer that I discovered Lucy Locket Loves and their funky leggings. I didn't want to wear Popsy dresses all the time, and I was fed up with jeans. I'd discovered the leggings earlier in the year when I was looking for running wear. I didn't at that point realise they sold casual leggings too. I was sold as soon as I spotted the music-themed leggings. I loved quite a few of the colourful and the purple-blue themed ones, so again, over time, I ended up with a collection of over thirty pairs. Novelty ones appeared too, including *Pac-Man*, rubber ducks and even *Tetris* (from an alternative company) more recently. I loved the designs with stars. Eventually, I started living in LLL leggings, and wearing Popsy dresses on days where I went live in my den.

At the end of August, we'd just come out of the first lockdown. I found my old, lost friend, Dean, and we met up for lunch with one other friend. We caught up on the missing years; it was bittersweet. It was the first time I'd gone out in public wearing Popsy. Alice was the dress I chose, and I knew I 'owned' it—no makeup, hair down, and my dress. It flattered my new figure perfectly. For the first time, I felt confident about how I looked.

It was also around then that I had a meltdown about money. I was terrified of using my savings because I'd be seen as a failure. It was my emergency funds, and I felt like a failure. I'd spent all the money on dresses and leggings rather than saving it because I'd lost so much already. I felt like I needed the dresses and leggings for my mental health. They were such positive colours, and they notably improved my confidence. Dr G, being his ever-supportive self, talked to me. Why was I so scared to dip into my savings? What is an emergency? If it stops you from going into debt or means you can pay off your credit card, just use it. You'll pay it back eventually. I needed that talk. He helped me feel like I could do this. I dipped into my savings. I was still terrified, but I felt a bit better knowing I could pay off my card. I just told myself not to do it unless I absolutely had to. I haven't had a meltdown about money since.

Between September and December 2020 was a sort of lull. We weren't in full lockdown, but people were careless and wary. September was the start of real change for me. In the real world, Michael had decided to return to do a postgraduate degree. He wanted me to be his assistant again, so I happily obliged. I was completely independent of the university this time. No way was I going back to work for that woman again. It turned out that most of his lectures were online, but over the term, we managed to get some in-person singing lessons in, with me as accompanist. It was a strange term, but we survived. I couldn't help but think he might have been better off staying at home in Canada than coming over to Wales. However, it was nice to be able to play the university's grand pianos once more and also be able to gain more experience as an accompanist whilst still vaguely in my comfort zone.

For that term, we were able to go back to face-to-face piano lessons too. Things were looking up. The laws in England and Wales were often different, and I'd given up trying to stay up to date. I was happy at home, and people were starting to notice my life a bit more.

In September, I came across More Than Just Mum. She'd just started out, and I was intrigued. I discovered her through the Vision Board Queen's group. As I got to know her, I found out she loved piano music and Tropic... amazing! She was also the same age as me, and it was nice to come across someone who had lots in common with me. I engaged in her group regularly and won a free discovery call at the end of October. That session had many lightbulb moments, and despite being scared of creating actual goals, she gave me plenty of things to think about. I think I needed that step up first before going back to the Vision Board Queen a bit later to try the more visual side of it.

It was late October that I started making my first lot of goals. I wanted to do a full live Christmas concert in my group. That would be my biggest goal of 2020. However, I decided to do a test run at the end of November first. I also planned a Twelve Days of Christmas special in my group for December. Every day had a fact about me, the relevant verse from the well-known Christmas carol, and my offer for the day. I planned a mix of purchase-based offers and free-to-enter games.

Earlier in November, I met up with Joan and Ruth from my original networking group. We'd built a friendship over the first lockdown, so it was great to be able to meet up in person. We went to a local restaurant, and I felt confident. It turned out Joan was anxious that day, and it felt strange to be the one who wasn't anxious, and I'd never actually been consciously in that situation before.

Later in the month, Dr G and I also met up with a couple of mutual friends for lunch. We went to a local chain pub as that was the only place we could find that was open. It was strange having to order everything via the app, but also so much more convenient. I wore my penguin Popsy dress that day, and later, when I went live on the piano for the first time ever. I was like a rabbit in headlights, and I forgot to flip my camera. I only realised when I read the comments back and someone had asked if I'd moved my piano! I played the 'Glasgow Love Theme' from *Love Actually* for that first session. It was perfect and sort of magical too. I was shaky, but I also observed that I wasn't as shaky as I was all those years ago when I last performed as a soloist at school.

Onwards to the Twelve Days of Christmas. I went live in my group every single morning for twelve days. A different Popsy dress each day, a different lip glaze and a fact about me. I played the piano, and I finished with my offer for the day. It did wonders for engagement, and people loved my games. Not all days were taken up, but that was assumed when planning as I couldn't afford to give away all the prizes I'd offered. It was completely exhausting, but I also loved every minute of it. The first day was nervous, but as the days went by, I got more confident.

Tropic HQ had just announced a big incentive. If I made a thousand pounds in sales for the first week of December, I'd win a luxury kit bag. When I first started back in March, I failed to win it, as although I got all my leap aheads, I couldn't do them quick enough to get the top prize. It was a second chance. I didn't know how I would do it, but I set my heart on that bag.

The first Saturday, I hosted a virtual duck race. I decided to commentate it. I'd just got myself some LLL rubber duck themed leggings by swapping a lucky dip. I got a good handful of people signing up, so for those ninety seconds, I tried my best to commentate. I'd never done anything like that before, so I ended up making random comments and feeling awkward. However, everyone loved it! After it finished, I reflected on it and realised I was getting somewhere properly with my confidence.

Over the twelve days, I also did two lots of Duck Duck Goose to get the engagement going more. The game of *Battleship* was the biggest hit. It was free to enter, and everyone had three guesses until they won something. The prizes took a while to get found, but so many people hopped on and attempted to win. I even posted in The Vision Board Queen's networking group to ask for support. The Vision Board Queen herself popped in, took a guess and won the star prize. She was as surprised as I was!

During that first week, Ian, who'd supported me since day one, came in with a massive Christmas order. I couldn't have done it without him, but his order, my prizes, plus everyone else s smaller orders added up, and I'd done it. I'd won the luxury kit bag. I was ecstatic! I'd never seriously chased an incentive before without stressing over it, but I was so happy I'd managed to do it this time. Usually, I barely scraped £250 in a month, so £1,000 in just over a week was phenomenal. My team congratulated me. It felt great, although half of me didn't believe it either. I wore my neon light LLL leggings that day and treated myself to an M&S lunch. I was so grateful for my community. People had emerged out of lurking status. Some new people had joined just as the Christmas campaign began, and I started to feel like people were starting to notice what I could offer them. The big live Christmas concert was the week after the Twelve Days of Christmas campaign had finished. I think I needed a week off to recover from the mental drain of the last week. It was all worth it, though.

On the day of the Christmas concert, Dr G and the kid went to his parents for the day, so I could prepare and be mentally ready for the huge plans of the afternoon! I saved my Elsa snowflake dress for this. I had custom-made earrings created by Joan, and I did my full makeup for the first time. I was shaking like a leaf when I started, but I introduced myself and got on with it. Most of the songs had been requested by customers who'd bought something over a set timeframe. It was great to be able to shout people out, and I took a couple of requests from my piano students too. There were a few mistakes here or there, but I got through it. I split the programme in half to make it more manageable, and by the time I got to my second half, I was confident. I saved the trickier pieces for the second half in case that happened, so I played it out perfectly. The feedback from that was breath-taking. So breath-taking, in fact, that I made a promise to go live every month in 2021. I'd learnt that I didn't need to be perfect to be a good pianist. I, therefore, was able to change my mindset into a confident pianist instead of the pianist that was afraid of failing. It was an amazing end to my businesses for 2020, but by Christmas, we were in lockdown again.

There's a debate about this. Was January 2021 lockdown two or three? It depended on which bit of the UK you lived in, but most called it lockdown three. To us, it was our second major lockdown, with the first one being

March to August 2020. This lockdown was from January to April. Everything shut again. Postponed events got postponed again. A poor couple we knew had their wedding postponed for the third time. My piano students went back online, I still didn't have to home-school, and Dr G had never stopped working from home, so nothing changed for him.

Before Christmas, Dr G had arranged for an extension to be built. The initial idea was that it would be his new office, and he wouldn't have to camp out at the dining table indefinitely. It was supposed to be finished by Christmas, but, of course, like most building works, everything got delayed. The weather was bad, and other urgent jobs came up. The builder was waiting for an electrician and plumber. As it started, Dr G decided that it was a new room for me. It had more space and was perfect as a piano studio, so that's what it was going to be. I was excited! I had no idea what to expect, but I knew that whatever it became, it would be better than what I had. I was lucky to have a study in the first place, but it was full of clutter and distractions, and I was convinced that it may have put some of my original enquiries off. All students were offered a free introductory session before starting. This vision was an exclusive studio, free of clutter, for teaching and business. It was gradual, with a lot of the main things not being done until March. The carpet was laid in April, and the piano and desk were moved over Easter weekend. The studio officially opened after the Easter break. It had to because I needed to teach from my piano. However, it wasn't until mid-May that the last part of the studio was finished. We'd been waiting for the radiator. It is indeed an exclusive studio. It was the first time I had a room that I could call my own, so naturally, I had purple skirting boards, silvery grey walls, and a purple-blue galaxy-themed feature wall.

In the January, we went back into lockdown again, but this lockdown was different. Being in bubbles meant we could officially use the grandparents as childcare properly again, and I allowed any vulnerable or smaller kids to come to in-person piano lessons. I was also a key worker this time, as I had Michael to support. The playgroup was shut until the week before Easter, but we survived. Like we had in the first lockdown, we got into a routine, scheduled ahead, knew exactly what we were doing one day to the next, and kept busy. While everyone was saying how slow January went, it went fast for me. I kept signing up for things again. I had piano lives to plan and goals to set.

I made a New Year's Resolution to start setting proper goals. I started small with things like: exercise a minimum of six times a week, watch a film, or read a book. I also added: do something outside of comfort zone and piano live session. I loved the Vision Board Queen's way of doing things, but it also wasn't quite me. She'd recommended a certain self-development book, *The Universe Has Your Back* by Gabby Bernstein. I'd read that before Christmas and found out that an attraction box was the same concept as a vision board, so I made one of those. I put my bigger goals in it, plus some motivational quotes. I still wasn't really connecting with it, though.

In January, I'd been following More Than Just Mum and saw how she set about doing things. She had a vision board, but she talked about smaller goals too. I decided to do monthly goals. Weekly seemed a bit overkill, and the big goals were out of reach for now. I ordered a notebook. It was dot-matrix just because I fancied something different. I started by doing abstract art. In January, I listed my goals, and when I achieved them, I'd draw a random shape and colour it in according to the colour I'd marked the point off with. It worked well. I carried that on, so February was hearts, March was flowers, April was eggs, May was ribbons, June was cupcakes, July was beach balls, August was sunshine, September was acorns, October was pumpkins, November was fireworks, and December had to be Christmas trees. At the end of the month, I shared it on my social media and tagged the two ladies who inspired me in the first place. By the end of 2021, I finished the year with a reel on Instagram to celebrate the first twelve months of setting goals and achieving them.

Also, in January, I started my *One Hundred Days of Happiness Journal.* It was from LLL and was full of prompts and journal entries, so I kept that until mid-April and then freestyled my own version. I wasn't as consistent with that over the summer, but I had been writing my blog. Later in 2021, I adapted the journal I'd used and made my own printed, spiral-bound, two-hundred-page journal exactly to my specification. I started my own stationery range from that, and it felt fantastic to have complete clarity on my brand.

As mentioned in my goals book, I set myself challenges to go out of my comfort zone every month. Every month in my den, I went live on the piano with two pieces. January was new, February I sang for the first time, March I played one of the fiddliest pieces I had, and April I dressed as a pirate! I also did a surprise mini piano session during the month too, including for Jazz Day, World Piano Day, and International Women's Day.

A lady I'd helped in November was the Visibility Queen. She popped up in the January, offering a virtual road trip starting in mid-February. I'd done so much social media training that I signed up for that as a change of scenery. It turned out to be the best decision I ever made. I'd spent the first lockdown working on my mindset, and despite various obstacles and adversities, I came out of the other side with confidence and no more fear of being judged.

The road trip taught me so much useful information, and from that, I was able to work out what my actual mission was. I wanted to set out to inspire and uplift people. The follow up to that was a thirty-day live challenge. I wasn't scared of it like some of the others were. I was mentally ready, even though the prospect of even going live in my private group terrified me just a year ago. For five minutes every day, I had to go live on my (public) Instagram account and talk about whatever the prompt was for the day. I loved every day. I always guessed the five minutes, so they were all a bit longer or shorter, except a couple that were spot on, but that didn't bother me. I tried to wear a different outfit for most of them, but I ended up wearing more casual things like hoodies rather than dresses or all black. I flashed my *Pac-man* leggings for one of them, wore a red nose, showed off my music, even played live piano for one of them. I was sad that they ended on thirty days, but the idea is it's supposed to make you comfortable for going live regularly going forward. I didn't do that. Not because I was scared. Simply because I had other things that I wanted to focus on. By the time March came round, the Visibility Queen was planning a charity event, and she asked me to be part of it. That was definitely out of my comfort zone, but I said yes straight away—my first gig as a pianist for the public outside of my own group.

I took part in collaborations for International Women's Day, and I networked like I always did. I made more connections, both new and old! I decided that March was the month I started working properly on visibility. March also marked one year since I became a Tropic Ambassador, and what a year it had been. I had worked so much on self-development that I felt it might be possible to overcome the whole anxiety disorder.

The charity event was at the end of March. It was phenomenal, and everyone watching absolutely loved my performance. I was shaky for the first piece. I played five different pieces live, and I was the first act who was performing. The rest of the artists were singers. After the first piece, I really got into it, so I worked out my programme like I had my Christmas one. Place the fiddly pieces after halfway in my programme. It worked like a dream.

We finally saw a light that we might be coming out of lockdown after Easter, but not before I was interviewed on YouTube by the Visibility Queen herself for her Blogbox. It was a fantastic experience, and it was my first go at being visible other than on my own platforms.

Summer was spent on the beach as much as possible. I had Tropic to keep me going, but the priority was spending some quality time with my child before he started full-time school in September. During August, I took requests in my den. Anyone who ordered that month could request whatever they liked. My favourites were 'Defying Gravity' from *Wicked* and 'Sleeping Sun' by *Nightwish.* Mia joined my team that month too. It came completely out of the blue, but she hoped to do it on the quiet. It was nice to have that connection with her again.

The new term started, and like any mother waving their child off on their first day at school, I was emotional at the school gate. I was proud but also nervous. He was much smaller than the other four year olds, and wasn't as advanced as they were. However, he was so bright with his language and is fully bilingual. He knows when to switch languages, even if he doesn't know as many words as his peers.

The first full week back at school also saw my first in-person networking event since lockdown. The Double V Celebration was a joint event hosted by my two heroes, The Visibility Queen and the Vision Board Queen. The faces at the event were familiar but strange at the same time. Many of us had met several times over Zoom but never in real life. My social anxiety was put to the test in real life for the first time. I was a bit nervous on entering the room, but once the hosts had greeted me, I knew I was in safe hands. I wore my favourite Ally Popsy dress with my starry hat. I was the most eccentrically dressed lady at the event, but everyone loved it, and I felt confident in myself for the first time. That day, I won the Queen of Progress award. I'd never won anything before. I was chuffed! I was also interviewed for my part in the collaboration book, *Seen.* It was launched in October 2021, and collectively we achieved best-seller status in six different categories across Amazon. My chapter was the first one in the book, and it was the perfect first step for what became this book.

I concluded 2021 by stepping up my live Christmas concert. I was featured in a local newspaper with a selfie of me holding my best-selling book, promoting my upcoming concert. I didn't spot the article until Christmas Eve, but it was still a moment worth celebrating.

I started my Christmas campaign in my den. This year I told a story with a Popsy dress and lipstick and sang a Victoria Wood inspired version of the 'Twelve Days of Christmas'. It wasn't as exhausting this time around, and I was confident from day one. I ended the campaign with the full live concert a week before Christmas, but this time it was for all who wished to attend. I sold tickets directly and had a goal in mind. Although I didn't quite achieve it, considering I had to private message everyone, I was proud of forty-one ticket sales. The feedback was out of this world for the second year in a row, and for some, I even made their Christmas!

'Invisible to Visible' was my theme for 2021.

THE YEAR OF THE TIGER

2022 is the Year of the Tiger. It is a powerful year, and it is my year. Through all of those years of being bullied, because I am half Chinese, I never forgot who I was. My heritage is fascinating. My childhood was different and learning to embrace that with everything else was the lesson I needed to take on my life's journey. The fear of judgement had held me back for so long it caused me to be afraid of everything at the peak of my Generalised Anxiety Disorder. It was a long and lonely tunnel heading for despair. The light from that tunnel came in the ironic form of lockdown. While everyone was locked away, my mind was able to open up and explore to find the life I truly wanted to live. I'm not just a mum or a wife. I'm a pianist and an adult gamer. I love my network marketing company, I'm passionate about communities, and best of all, I'm a writer. I needed to find my way to free myself from the trap of my own mind to enable me to be who I truly am. 2022 was the year I finally achieved not being anxious every hour of every day.

Now when presented with the question of, 'What will you do out of your comfort zone?', I will simply reply, 'What comfort zone?'

My sole purpose is to inspire and entertain people through my creativity and uniqueness, whether through my writing, music, or my unique style.

ACKNOWLEDGEMENTS

I'd like to thank my husband, Dr G, for always being by my side. We balance each other out perfectly, and he was the calm to my anxiety. We were always the dream team and always will be.

Thank you to his family for supporting and understanding me from the beginning.

Thank you to Mrs Johnson for being the inspirational piano tutor that I aspired to be one day.

Thank you to James and Beth, for believing in me from the day we met and enabling me to grow the hub to its full potential (eventually). Thank you to the other founders, without whom we couldn't have built such a thriving hub.

Thank you to Stacey for giving me the opportunity to begin to tell my story.

I'd also like to thank Kat Massey, the Visibility Queen. Without her, I wouldn't have had the opportunity to be a bestseller in the first place, nor the opportunities to reach further and stay out of my comfort zone.

Thanks to Lisa Williams, the Vision Board Queen, and Heather Palfreyman, More Than Just Mum, for getting me started on my journey of clarity and goal setting.

Thank you to my local MIB (Mum's in Business), Anglesey (& Gwynedd), for supporting me in my earlier days as a business owner.

A particular thank you to Kim; my kid may have stolen your toast on the first day, but it's because of you that I found my place in the world and a strategy to grow with.

Thank you also to Jackie and Fiona for being my cheerleaders from day one of networking.

Thank you to Daniel, Sue and John for putting your trust in me and particularly to Daniel for showing me how to stand up for what's right. We supported each other through some of the hardest times, and we came out on top.

Thank you to Chris and Anna. The old friends who supported me from the start of my network marketing journey. It means a lot.

And a final thank you to my own family. Without you, I wouldn't have found my passion for music in the first place. Your hearts were always in the right place, and for that, I am grateful.

ABOUT THE AUTHOR

Jen is known as the Tropic Pianist Gamer and lives on Anglesey with her husband and child.

She grew up in the shadows of Greater Manchester, having a fascinating upbringing being half Chinese. A talented musician from a young age, she had many hobbies, too many, in fact. Anything creative was right up her street, including colourful and fun video games. In the background, she was always journaling, writing poetry, songs or the occasional novel. The school implied she wasn't good enough as a writer, so she hid her content for many years. She believes that writing helped her through some of the most stressful parts of her life.

Having anxiety problems from the age of thirteen but not being diagnosed with Generalised Anxiety Disorder until the age of twenty-seven, there left a gap where mental health was brushed under the carpet, and she was seen as weak.

After trying counselling, CBT, mindfulness and other conventional methods, it took a life-changing event to instigate change. After creating a network that offered encouragement and support, Jen realised by telling her story, she could help others.

https://tropicpianistgamer.co.uk

Facebook: @tropicpianistgamer
Instagram: @tropicpianistgamer

Printed in Great Britain
by Amazon

42654435R00155